Endorsements

The ministry of deliverance was scarcely performed in the Old Testament. It was introduced when Jesus came as our deliverer, and the early church continued in the ministry of deliverance after Jesus died and rose again. However, in much of today's ministry, deliverance has become like it was in the Old Testament: scarcely done. Many spiritual leaders and parishioners are being tormented, and the fact is that they haven't been delivered. Many of them don't even truly know that what they're facing is demonic. This is the reason Apostle Gloire E. Ndongala wrote this book on deliverance, which I believe is one of the most important topics for the church today. *Deliver Us* enlightens us about the need for the body of Christ to embrace deliverance, as it was one of the most important facets of Jesus' ministry. This book will help you find freedom for yourself and help lead others into freedom as well.

-Dr. Ansy Dessources, author and pastor of Healing Center Community Church

The Word of God is living and active (Hebrews 4:12). This means I can read the same passage today, tomorrow, and next week, and the Lord can use it to speak to me differently each time. It will always be exactly what I need!

This has also been the effect of *Deliver Us* by Apostle Gloire Emmanuel Ndongala. Apostle Gloire teaches on the spiritual realm and uses the holy Scriptures to substantiate the need for a modern-day response to spiritual oppression. The teaching follows very closely with Scripture, referencing the Bible often as well as interweaving personal accounts and testimonies. It is a power-packed teaching that the church needs to hear. The amount of spiritual activity in the world is at a fever pitch, and as the prevalence of wickedness increases, so does the amount of grace and anointing God releases through His servants. He came to set the captive free, and we are His hands and feet! I am excited for every reader of this book because I know this moment has been ordained for your healing and liberation. Lord, Deliver Us! Amen!

- Pastor Brandon Morgan, Church Home Conroe (Conroe, TX.)

I struggled with homosexuality for over 25 years and the churches I attended never fully addressed how to get out of the lifestyle. When I turned 30, I decided to start talking about my struggle and seeking help. Within six months, God led me to meet this amazing man of God who openly talked about how God had delivered him from homosexuality and pornography. It was a miracle-I had finally met someone who not only understood what I was going through, but also provided hope for a way out of it: deliverance through the power of the Holy Spirit.

Gloire took me through deliverance, and I felt demons leave my body through my shoulders and hands. As I've continued to experience the sanctifying work of God since then, I have developed a fire in my heart to spread hope to the lost and especially to the LGBTQ+ community. Jesus wants to make us whole again as we break spiritual ties. He commissioned us to preach the gospel, and that "these signs [would] accompany those who believe; in [His] name [we] will cast out demons…" (Mark 16:17). This book will help you be equipped to do that effectively!

-Kyle Pettis

Demonic oppression is real. Satan and his crew have not revised/updated their objective, which is to fight human beings. The world wants to give us the impression that demons only operate in Third World countries and not in developed countries (the western world). The truth is that Satan works differently depending on what part of the world he is in, but at the core, he still wants to achieve the same objective.

This book will help you understand how demons oppress people and will equip you with knowledge that enables you to identify doors and gates through which demons have access into your life. Gloire's heart, which is seen clearly through this book, is that nobody would live under the oppression of demons.

-Pastor Bellarmee Milosi, clergy in the United Methodist Church

Gloire shares the authentic need for deliverance both inside and outside of the church today. I felt the Holy Spirit minister to me through this book, and I recognize and honor the the anointing on Gloire's life. He has a desire to express the truth of God's Word on this topic to see people truly healed and set free through the truth and the power of God. I pray that as you listen, read, and apply the truths shared in this book, the Holy Spirit will minister to you and set you completely free! May this catapult and equip you to also help others be set free in the much-needed ministry of deliverance! For the kingdom and for God's glory, let it be done!!!

- Pastor Rebecca Morgan, Church Home Conroe (Conroe, TX.)

As I read through this incredible book about deliverance, I can honestly say that I've never seen such a biblically exhaustive account of Satan's function on the earth. This book biblically and historically exposes, expounds, equips, and informs us in an easy-to-read manner who the devil and his demons are and how they operate in the lives of both believers and unbelievers.

This is a subject that many churches have stayed away from, whether out of fear or ignorance. However, I truly believe the Lord has selected Gloire for such a time as this, as the demonic is becoming normal (paganism, witchcraft, etc.), to wake up and prepare the western church to return to the deliverance ministry of Jesus and the apostles.

-Matt Daniels

I always assumed that deliverance ministry was either purely cultural or rooted in superstition. This assumption, as it turned out, was due to my own ignorance and biblical illiteracy. After walking through deliverance with my husband, I experienced freedom from a mental stronghold that I'd been unable to overcome since childhood. *Deliver Us* is a product of years of in-depth Bible study, practical ministry experience, and revelation from the Holy Spirit. This book gives biblical context and language to deliverance and connects the semantics of multiple cultures, making it a great resource for practically understanding and applying the ministry of deliverance.

-Katie Ndongala

Deliver Us is an insightful and revelatory book. Gloire does an incredible job bringing clarity to the ministry of deliverance, identifying the need for it, and explaining the origin of spiritual powers in the kingdom of darkness. I also appreciate the prayers he provides at the end of each chapter. This is a must-read because many people are perishing due to a lack of knowledge. *Deliver Us* helps address this need by eradicating deception and providing the pathway to freedom through Jesus Christ.

-Dr. Stacey Jones

Gloire is a man of God. I can think of no greater praise than this. I have watched Gloire minister the love of God and the freedom of God to others and have had the privilege of ministering with him. He is passionate about seeing others get free from bondage, stay free, and walk in their God-given identity. He exemplifies the love of God in his ministry, his preaching, and his writing. I am honored to call him a friend and to see him continue to bless others. I believe this book, *Deliver Us*, will bless many across the earth and further the Kingdom of God. Listen to the Holy Spirit speak as you read this book and allow the love and freedom of God to flow into your life. I pray that the love of God, Father, Son, and Holy Spirit, will flow through you into the lives of those you love and those you will love as you minister to them.

-Rod Kopp, Associate Pastor, Antioch Church, Great Falls, MT

Deliver Us

A Guide to Spiritual Freedom

by Gloire Emmanuel Ndongala

Deliver Us
A Guide to Spiritual Freedom

Authors contact details:
Email: gloire@gloirendongala.com
Website: gloirendongala.com
TikTok: Gloire777
YouTube: Gloire Ndongala
Instagram: Gloire777
Facebook: Gloire Emmanuel Ndongala

Published by Gloire Emmanuel Ndongala

ISBN: 979-8-9856473-8-9

For the Glory of God.

Dedication

I would like to thank my Lord and Savior Jesus Christ for the inspiration for this book. To Katie, my best friend, for supporting me in my writing journey. To Jean Cazy, for teaching me about deliverance. To Jason Rutel for the cover, and to Kelani Daniels for editing. Lastly, I'd like to thank my spiritual father, Dr. Ansy Dessources, for believing in me.

Table of Contents

Preface

When I was 23, I became hungry to know and walk in the call of God for my life. I had just become engaged to be married, and while I knew I was called to do ministry, I didn't know what this ministry was or when it was going to start.

One day, my spiritual mother invited a prophet from India to her house, and a lot of students from our university went to hear him. When I showed up, I immediately noticed a long line of people waiting to get a prophetic word from this man of God. In my heart, I told God, *I want to know when I'm going to walk out my calling. I know you've called me to the nations, but I wanna know when I'm supposed to go. Can you please tell me when I'm supposed to go?*

I finally made it to the front of the line. The prophet looked at me and said, "Six years from now your ministry is going to start. Around the same time Jesus' ministry started, your ministry is going to start."

Six years later, I found myself living in Cut Bank, Montana. My wife and I had started a church plant and flew in one of my best friends, Jean Cazy, to minister. On the first night of ministry, Jean taught about how demons oppress Christians.

Jean prayed for different people, and as he did, he exposed the demonic spirits that were dwelling in them by having the people interlock their fingers. He would then command every demonic spirit that was in those people to reveal themselves in the name of Jesus by causing them to not be able to pull their hands apart. To all our amazement, their hands would be locked (Demons being exposed link: https://youtu.be/9VHiTMc9wyk). He would tell them to try to unlock them, and they would either struggle to pull them apart or they wouldn't be able to open them at all until he commanded the demons to release their hands.

Many of those watching this take place were amazed at what they saw. Others were shocked, and I was shocked right alongside them. After seeing this, many people came and asked to be delivered.

Jean ended up taking a person out of the sanctuary to do a one-on-one deliverance session with them. My other two friends who were there with us, Stacey and Matt, were also learning all this deliverance stuff with me.

I was standing there, still trying to understand what had just happened, when a lady who had been involved in witchcraft came up to me for prayer. I told her to put her hands together like I'd just seen Jean do, and I commanded every demonic spirit to reveal itself by locking her hands. She had great difficulty unlocking her hands. I prayed with her a bit more, and Jean came to check on my progress. I asked her if she was okay with Jean taking her through deliverance in front of the church so that people could learn, and she agreed.

Jean had to leave briefly to pray for someone outside the sanctuary, so I attempted to buy him some time by asking this lady questions on the mic. I hoped to also use the moment as a teaching opportunity. I was hoping Jean would be gone for just a few minutes, but he did not return.

Suddenly, I felt the gentle impression of the Holy Spirit on my heart, prompting me to take her through deliverance. I thought to myself, *me?* But I knew it was God speaking to me, so I had to obey. I looked at the lady and asked her to repeat after me and renounce (confess) her sins. I let her know that we would then denounce her sins (nullify every consequence that was taking place in her life).

"Repeat after me," I said. "Say, 'every demonic spirit,'".

"Every denomic…denomic…" She could not say "demonic" correctly. Some people gasped, and others had a look of excitement as they witnessed the power of God on display for the first time. After trying again to say "demonic" correctly and failing, I asked everyone in the crowd to stretch their hands towards her and pray with me that the devil would loosen her tongue.

As we prayed, you could visibly see the spiritual warfare as the lady's physical body began to move backward as though she was going to fall. I invited a friend of mine to stand behind her in case she did. I continued to command the demonic spirits to loosen her tongue and to come out until I sensed a release from the Spirit of God.

I had her again attempt to repeat after me and say, "Every demonic spirit," and this time she said it perfectly. Everyone in the congregation began to clap their hands, glorifying God for what He had done. I continued praying for her until Jean came back. A good portion of her deliverance session was filmed on FacebookLive and has been uploaded to YouTube. Here is the link: https://youtu.be/qQGv0IAQbMY.

A few months later, my wife and I went to Texas and met up with one of our college professors, Dr. Gary Royer, who had taught us about the spiritual world. I told him about everything that had taken place. I shared about how peoples' hands were getting stuck together in the name of Jesus and I wanted to make sure that I wasn't going off the deep end or operating in error.

He looked at me and said, "Gloire, as long as you don't make this the only method of deliverance, I don't see anything wrong with it because people are being set free." This was my final confirmation. I knew from that moment on that this was the ministry Jesus had called me to.

When the Canaanite woman approached Jesus in Matthew 15 and told Him her daughter was demon-possessed, the disciples urged her to go away. Jesus also spoke to her and said, "I was sent only to the lost sheep of Israel" (Matthew 15:24 NIV).

But the Canaanite woman begged Jesus again for help. Jesus again responded unfavorably, saying, "It is not right to take the children's bread and toss it to the dogs" (Matthew 15:26 NIV). However, this woman was not going to let Jesus go.

She said, "Yes it is, Lord. Even the dogs eat the crumbs that fall from their master's table" (Matthew 15:27 NIV). Jesus was amazed by her faith and replied, "Woman, you have great faith! Your request is granted." And from that moment, her daughter was healed (Matthew 15:28 NIV).

Many people normally quote this passage when praying for healing, saying "healing is the children's bread". If we read this contextually, however, we discover that included in the "children's bread", what God has provided for us, is deliverance. This bread is for all of us. We all need Jesus to Deliver Us.

Chapter 1

AFRICA

~~~

Before I was born, doctors had told my mom that she couldn't have any more kids. My mom believed in miracles, though, and so I was born, despite professional opinions. I was a miracle baby.

The Democratic Republic of Congo was no easy place to raise a child. The Congo was and is a land filled with the practices of spiritism, witchcraft, sorcery, and superstitions, making it both a spiritually and physically dangerous environment.

When I was about four years old, I was hanging out in the streets with some of my friends and was introduced to a new fad that was growing in popularity. Many people were cutting their arms on the back of their wrists--three slits across each arm with a razor blade and then "invoking" a power. Their eyes would roll back behind their heads, and they would close their hands, making fists on the sides of their bodies.

Then they would swing their right hand up to their face diagonally, followed by their left, as if they were doing a martial art move. They would
~~~

repeat this for about 20 seconds. Then they would square off like you see in old Western movies. There would be two people, each about 20 feet apart, staring at one another, hands at their sides like they were about to draw their pistols.

That evening as I witnessed this for the first time, everyone fell silent and watched, waiting to see what would happen next. Each "fighter" would robotically bring up their preferred hand and point it at the other person while making a gun shape with their hand. We all watched as they fired at one another with invisible "bullets".

These bullets were invisible, yet you could tell when someone was hit because after each "shot" that was fired, a scratch mark would appear on the person right where they had been "shot". They went back and forth until one person eventually gave up.

After watching this, my friends and I went back to my house and started imitating what we'd seen. We used ashes to mark three lines on the opposite sides of our wrists, just like they did, and we started moving back, clenching our fists to our sides. The last thing we needed to do was to "invoke" the power.

That's when my mom walked in.

"What are you doing?" she yelled, grabbing my hand. "Are you practicing witchcraft like I told you not to?"

Our house had cement walls about six feet high enclosed all around it. There was a church that met in our front yard, and occasionally they would throw a potluck party. Unfortunately for me, this was one of those potluck days…the day I chose to conjure up demons.

My mom brought me into our yard, which was full of people. My heart was pounding. *Man, for sure I'm going to die,* I thought. I knew she wasn't going to let me off easily.

I grew up under the reign of Mobutu, during the time when the Democratic Republic of the Congo was called Zaire. Simply put, this was no democracy. You could be put to death even for stealing, even though our constitution encouraged it.

Jail in Zaire was not a place where you got three meals a day. It was a death sentence no matter what the accused person did. For this reason and many others, almost every parent was extremely strict with their children. They felt that if they didn't discipline hard, their children could end up dead.

My mom fully believed in hard discipline, so when she caught me doing something that society deemed punishable by death, she felt obligated to teach me a lesson I'd would never forget.

On this day, she took a brick, put me in a corner, and said, "Lift this brick above your head. If you dare drop it, I'm going to whip you." So there I was shirtless and malnourished, trying to hold a brick above my head. My arms began to shake, my knees began to buckle, and it seemed like I had been holding the brick up for an eternity.

My mom commanded my uncle to watch me. If I dropped the brick, she said, he had the right to spank me. I looked at him with the most pitiful face I could for about 30 seconds. I was beginning to sweat, and my eyes were starting to water. My arms were getting weaker and weaker, and the brick was becoming stronger than me. One minute approached and I knew I was as good as whipped-the brick was now level with my forehead. My uncle moved his feet and I struggled to push the brick back up quickly.

Two minutes.

I couldn't take it anymore. Everybody from the neighborhood was there eating and I could smell the delicious food. I thought to myself, *I will never try to invoke some demonic power again*. Fortunately, a lady from the church saw me and said, "Bea, I think he learned his lesson."

She came and relieved me of the brick. My arms hurt so bad! I could barely lift them up. My mom looked at me and said, "You know, those people who are doing these things normally have to pay a heavy price to receive their powers. Some of them even kill their own family members." I stared at her in shock.

I remembered what some of the kids who'd come out of that lifestyle said about how they murdered their family members just to have that kind of power. They would sacrifice them to the devil and even eat their flesh. The people who did this witchcraft and sorcery were called, in my language, "ba ndoki," which means "sorcerers" or "witches."

However, sometimes the Congolese people, because of their fear, would take measures into their own hands and have witch hunts. I've seen families be torn apart and children be burned in tires all because they were believed to have demons in them.

As I grew older and got saved, I began to question the way some believers handled witches in the Congo. If the Jesus whom they talked about so much died for everyone who was a sinner, then why were some of the Christians taking matters into their own hands and killing sinners? Didn't Jesus come to deliver us from evil?

Chapter 2

A MOVING SHADOW

~~~

It's been said that it's harder to find atheists in Africa because desperate living conditions cause Africans to seek supernatural help. Another reason is that supernatural activity in Africa is common knowledge.

Most people in Africa either know someone who has had encounters with the spirit world, or you yourself had encounters. There was no in-between. These encounters were good sometimes and very dark most of the time. I saw countless things while in the Congo that would cause many people to question everything they've believed about the supernatural world.

I had my own encounters starting when I was about 3 years old.
I used to sleep next to my grandma when I was little but one day, I wanted to sleep next to my mom. I used to call my mom ‘Auntie Bea’ because I called my grandma ‘mom’.

That night neither my mom nor I slept. I started seeing a shadow moving in her room. My mom could not see it, but I could.
~~~

Every time it moved, I'd point to the part of the room it was in and say, “It’s over their Auntie Bea!” My mom would then go to where that corner was and start praying. This went on all night long.

By the time morning came my mom was exhausted. My mom told me when I was older that I had seen this shadow in the morning leave the room and go out beyond our fenced yard. Yet even then, she said, I tried to chase after it but my grandparents stopped me before I left our walled yard.

My mom during this event couldn't really understand what was going on. Since we built a church in our front yard, men of God would normally come for prayer in the mornings. When my mom saw them, she told them about what had happened all night.

They immediately went into the living room and started to pray. Not too long into their prayer, they heard a noise in the ceiling. Suddenly, a giant lizard fell from inside the ceiling and slammed onto the table where the men of God were praying. It was like something from a horror movie!

They all jumped backward, their faces etched with shock and disbelief. They took the lizard and burned it. This giant lizard probably could have hurt me, but God rescued me from what was meant to be an attack of Satan.

Unfortunately, I’ve found that many people would brush off something like this as untrue or merely a “natural occurrence”. As an African who came to live in America, it has never ceased to amaze me that supernatural occurrences seemed to be rarer in America than they were in Africa. God is not a different god in every country, but the understanding of who He is can vary from one country to the next.

For years, I would ponder on why I saw so much supernatural in Africa that I hardly saw in America. I would fast in hope of seeing God move supernaturally, and though I grew through these times of fasting and seeking the Lord, I still would feel like something was missing. But what was it?

After years of searching and praying, and of experiencing both the church in the western world and the church in the eastern world, one day the Holy Spirit gave me a revelation. I realized there was one main reason why the eastern church was experiencing the tangible move of God's spirit and the western church seemed to be experiencing very little of it. It had to do with the true definition of the word *salvation*.

Prayer

Father, You said in Your Word, "At just the right time, I heard you. On the day of salvation, I helped you." Indeed, the "right time" is now. Today is the day of salvation (2 Corinthians 6:2 NLT). I want today to be my day of salvation. Jesus, I am a sinner in need of your grace and mercy. I have broken the Ten Commandments and have lived according to the flesh. Today I want to completely surrender my life to you. I confess with my mouth that You are Lord and I believe that You, Jesus, died on the cross and rose on the third day. Today I'm inviting you to come into my heart and be my Lord and my Savior. In Jesus' name, amen.

Chapter 3

SALVATION

In Greek, the word for salvation is sótéria (so-tay-ree'-ah), which means "welfare, prosperity, deliverance, preservation, salvation, and safety". It comes from the root word *sṓzō,* which means "to save and rescue". Salvation refers to God's rescue of humanity, which delivers believers out of destruction and into His safety[1].

To truly understand what happens when we're saved, let's first look at *why* we must be saved. In Genesis 3, we read the story about the fall of man. Prior to this, God had told Adam that the day he disobeyed, "dying he would surely die" מֹ֥ות תָּמֽוּת Mowt-Tamut (Genesis 2:15-17 Young's Literal Translation).

Following the fall, Adam lived to be 930 years old. However, because of the sinful actions of Adam and Eve, anyone born after them would be born with sin in their DNA. David, in Psalm 51, acknowledged the reality of being born into sin. "Behold, I was brought forth in iniquity, and in sin did my mother conceive me" (Psalm 51:5).

Conceived and deceived-deception embedded itself deep into mankind. Our hearts became exceedingly wicked. According to Jeremiah 17:9, "the human heart is the most deceitful of all things, and desperately wicked. Who really knows how bad it is?" (NLT)

Our sinful nature guaranteed our demise. Human beings went from being full of life to being dead in their trespasses.

> "And you were dead in the trespasses and sins in which you once walked, following the course of this world, following the prince of the power of the air, the spirit that is now at work in the sons of disobedience— among whom we all once lived in the passions of our flesh, carrying out the desires of the body and the mind, and were by nature children of wrath, like the rest of mankind. But God, being rich in mercy, because of the great love with which he loved us, even when we were dead in our trespasses, made us alive together with Christ—by grace you have been saved— and raised us up with him and seated us with him in the heavenly places in Christ Jesus" (Ephesians 2:1-6).

This passage in Ephesians clearly identifies what transpired with mankind because of sin. Yet, it also gives us the solution: *but God.* With no way of delivering ourselves out of bondage, we became like the dead man in 2 Kings 13:20.

> "So Elisha died, and they buried him. Now bands of Moabites used to invade the land in the spring of the year. And as a man was being buried, behold, a marauding band was seen and the man was thrown into the grave of Elisha, and as soon as the man touched the bones of Elisha, he revived and stood on his feet" (2 Kings 13:20-21).

Just like this man, all of humanity was headed to the pit with no way of saving themselves. Dead men cannot bring themselves back to life. But unexpectedly, this man's dead body was thrown into the burial tomb of the man of God, Elisha, whose name means "God is my salvation". When the dead man's body touched the bones of Elisha, which still had residue from the Spirit of God on them, the dead man was resurrected.

Elisha had to die so this man could come to life. In the same manner, Jesus, whose name means "savior" in line with Elisha's name, came and died in our place and reversed the curse that was on us by becoming a curse for us. As the Scriptures state, "Christ redeemed us from the curse of the law by becoming a curse for us—for it is written, "Cursed is everyone who is hanged on a tree"— (Galatians 3:13).

The Reverse Curse

In John 3:3, Jesus told Nicodemus that no man could ever see or enter the Kingdom of God unless they were born again. Nicodemus thought Jesus was speaking about physical birth, but Jesus clarified that what He spoke about had to do with the Spirit (John 3:4-17). This is what I call *the reverse curse.*

A curse came upon mankind in the Old Testament as a result of the fall, and man became separated from God. This is known as spiritual death, where humankind was left with a soul that was dying and a body that would die. Jesus came and He reversed this curse of sin that brought about death.

> "Therefore, just as sin came into the world through one man, and death through sin, and so death spread to all men because all sinned— For if,

> because of one man's trespass, death reigned through that one man, much more will those who receive the abundance of grace and the free gift of righteousness reign in life through the one man Jesus Christ. Therefore, as one trespass led to condemnation for all men, so one act of righteousness leads to justification and life for all men. For as by the one man's disobedience the many were made sinners, so by the one man's obedience the many will be made righteous" (Romans 5:12, 17-19).

When Jesus enters a person's heart during salvation (Romans 10:9-12; Ephesians 2:8-9), that person's spirit comes to life immediately and is brand new. This is known as justification, which means "just as if I didn't do it" (Romans 5:1; Ephesians 1). Their soul, however, is in the *process* of being renewed, which is called sanctification (Acts 26:18; Romans 12:1-2; 2 Thessalonians 2:13).

Eventually, the person's body will be new, for we all will get a new body one day, untainted by sin's corruption. This is called glorification (Philippians 3:21; 1 Corinthians 15:35-50; 2 Corinthians 5:1-10; Revelation 21:1-4).

Three in One

> "Now may the God of peace himself sanctify you completely, and may your whole spirit and soul and body be kept blameless at the coming of our Lord Jesus Christ. He who calls you is faithful; he will surely do it." (1 Thessalonians 5:23-24)

The human being is created in the image of a God, Elohim, who is three in one.

> "Then God said, "Let us make man in our image, after our likeness. And let them have dominion over the fish of the sea and over the birds of the heavens and over the livestock and over all the earth and over every creeping thing that creeps on the earth." So God created man in his own image, in the image of God he created him; male and female he created them" (Genesis 1:26-27).

The *us* and *our* in this verse is clearly speaking of God-He made us in His image. As we will see throughout the Bible, there are three persons in the godhead, yet they are one: God the Father, God the Son, and God the Holy Spirit. There is a heavenly council that exists, but as we read later on in Genesis, man is not made in the image of the heavenly council but the image of God. Scripture states, "Whoever sheds the blood of man, by man shall his blood be shed, for God made man in his own image" (Genesis 9:6).

In this verse, God is reaffirming what He'd previously stated in Genesis 1:26-27. The term "own image" in this verse confirmedly identifies what image man bears. In light of this, we as humans are three in one. We have a spirit, which is our inner being- the breath of God. These attributes are embedded in our spirit being: wisdom or intuition, conscience (conviction when we're saved), and communion (desire to fellowship) (Job 38:36; Rom 2:15; 13:5; 1 Cor. 8:7, 10, 12; 10:25, 27, 28, 29; 2 Cor. 4:2; 5:11; 1 Tim. 1:5, 19; 3:9; 4:2; 2 Tim. 1:31; John 16:8; 1 John 1).

Then we have a soul, which is our cognition (mind), volition (will), and our emotions. The last part of us is our body. The following verses in the Old

Testament show the difference between all three parts of us. "And the LORD God formed man of the dust of the ground and breathed into his nostrils the breath of life; and man became a living soul" (Genesis 2:7).

The following is the Hebrew iteration of Genesis 2:7:

וַיִּיצֶר֩ יְהוָ֨ה אֱלֹהִ֜ים אֶת־הָֽאָדָ֗ם עָפָר֙ מִן־הָ֣אֲדָמָ֔ה וַיִּפַּ֥ח בְּאַפָּ֖יו נִשְׁמַ֣ת חַיִּ֑ים וַֽיְהִ֥י הָֽאָדָ֖ם לְנֶ֥פֶשׁ חַיָּֽה׃

- מִן־הָ֣אֲדָמָ֔ה means "the dust of the ground"
- לְנֶ֥פֶשׁ means "Nephesh soul" (creature)
- נִשְׁמַ֣ת means "breathed spirit" (nishmat)

Another place in Scripture that shows the division of spirit, soul, and body is found in the book of Hebrews. Hebrews 4 states the following about the Word of God:

> "For the word of God is living and active and sharper than any double-edged sword, and piercing as far as the division of soul and spirit, both joints and marrow, and able to judge the reflections and thoughts of the heart" (Hebrews 4:12 LEB).

According to this passage, God's Word cuts between soul, spirit, joints and marrow. Here, then, we see that the spirit, soul, and the body each can be divided, further supporting that we are, indeed, three in one.

Salvation is both an instant position and a progressive action. It's instant in that when we get saved, we are immediately a new creature. Second Corinthians 5:17 states that if anyone is in Christ, "he is a new creation. The old has passed away; behold, the new has come". Indeed, the old has passed and the new has come in our spiritual being, but our soul and body will remain in a process of sanctification and glorification.

Being a new creature does not mean we are made entirely perfect once we are saved, but rather, that we are being perfected. The Bible is clear that we are not fully perfected at salvation, as we are still told we must repent of sin.

> "If we say we have no sin, we deceive ourselves, and the truth is not in us. If we confess our sins, he is faithful and just to forgive us our sins and to cleanse us from all unrighteousness" (1 John 1:8-9).

Along the same lines, Paul wrote to the church of Galatia, letting them know that "for freedom Christ has set us free; stand firm therefore, and do not submit again to a yoke of slavery" (Galatians 5:1). Truly, Christ has set us free from our sin, and yet we can, at times, fall back to our sinfulness.

Are there consequences when we do fall back into our sinfulness, since we are saved? According to Ephesians 4, there are.

> "Therefore, putting away lying, "Let each one of you speak truth with his neighbor," for we are members of one another. 'Be angry, and do not sin': do not let the sun go down on your wrath, nor give place to the devil" (Ephesians 4:25-27 NKJV).

Paul made it clear that if they opened the door to sin, they would give the devil a place. This "place" refers to an actual place in their being. It's not a place in their spirit because that is new, but rather in their soul and body, which is still in a process.

How can the devil live in a person's soul? And what are the ramifications of this? Let's look at some examples. How many believers do you know are living in unforgiveness? Many people don't realize how detrimental this sin is and that it has the capacity to open the door to mental and physical illness.

Another huge sin the devil comes into the soul through is sexual immorality. Here are a few astonishing stats on pornography in the church:

- 47% of families in the US have reported porn to be a problem in their home.
- Pornography use increases the marital infidelity rate by more than 300%.
- The average age that a child is first exposed to porn is 11, and 94% of children will see porn by the age of 14.
- 56% of American divorces involve one party having an "obsessive interest" in pornographic websites.
- 70% of Christian youth pastors report that they've had at least one teen come to them for help in dealing with pornography in the past 12 months.
- 68% of church-going men and over 50% of pastors view porn on a regular basis. Of young Christian adults 18-24 years old, 76% actively search for porn.
- 59% of pastors said that married men seek their help for porn use.
- Only 13% of self-identified Christian women say they never watch porn—87% of Christian women have watched porn.
- 57% of pastors say porn addiction is the most damaging issue in their congregation. 69% say porn has adversely impacted the church" [2]

How is it that a new creation in Christ is still falling into this level of impurity? Should we say that people watching pornography are not saved? Or are they being spiritually attacked because of spiritual doors that are open in their lives?

I believe they are being spiritually attacked because of spiritual doors that are open in their lives. Many of those struggling with pornography wish they were able to be free from it, but they feel stuck. If they understood that it's not just their flesh they're fighting, but Satan's demonic agents, it would help them know what to fight and relieve them of guilt and condemnation.

Many mistakenly believe that once they're in Christ, they aren't supposed to battle these things anymore, so they end up thinking they're evil instead of believing that they're new creations. Yet, many times, people in these situations are averse to the idea that they could need deliverance.

I've discovered that people often resist deliverance for the following reasons:

- lack of concrete biblical teachings
- fear
- unmet expectations
- ignorance
- no biblical understanding of the concept of deliverance
- thinking deliverance should be a certain way
- skepticism and doubt
- religiosity
- control
- a lack of belief the Spirit of God is still active today.

Yet people need to be free! There are countless believers who live day to day tormented by the devil. I believe it's time for us to be willing to put aside any false things we may have believed about deliverance so we can experience the joy and the freedom Jesus paid for us to have.

Prayer

Holy Spirit, I invite you to come. The Bible says, "When the Spirit of truth comes, he will guide you into all the truth, for he will not speak on his own authority, but whatever he hears he will speak, and he will declare to you the things that are to come" (John 16:13). Spirit of truth. I invite you to open my eyes to the truth about deliverance. I don't just want to gain man's wisdom, but I want to know Your perspective on the matter. Help me to discover the truth. Jesus, teach me Your ways so I can grow and be more like You! Reveal what the enemy has caused to be sealed in me. Open up the eyes of my heart. In your name I pray, amen!

Chapter 3 Questions

1. What is the word salvation in Greek? What is the definition?

2. Why does humanity need salvation?

3. What is the process of salvation?

4. According to the author, human beings are composed of how many parts? What are these parts?

5. Mankind was made in the image of who? How do we know?

Chapter 4

MY FIRST ENCOUNTER WITH THE HOLY SPIRIT

~~~

We’re first introduced to the Holy Spirit (ךוּחַ הַקֹּדֶשׁ Ru•ach Ha•kó•desh) in the first few verses of the Bible. Genesis 1:2 says, “The earth was without form and void, and darkness was over the face of the deep. And the Spirit of God was hovering over the face of the waters”. The Spirit of God has a way of showing up in places that are formless, void, and filled with darkness. He gives form to the formless, fills the emptiness with life, and lights up the darkness.

David stated, “When you send forth your Spirit, they are created, and you renew the face of the ground” (Psalm 104:30). When God’s Spirit comes, we are molded, our emptiness gets filled, and the darkness we carry inside gets banished. True deliverance only comes through the Spirit of God!

I once had an open vision of the Holy Spirit delivering people from deep darkness. I was around twelve years old and was not a believer. My mom had dragged us to a prayer meeting at one of her friend’s houses in Denver. We entered the house and went downstairs to the basement, which was big enough to seat thirty people.
~~~

The pastor leading this meeting told everyone to find their seats, close their eyes, and pray. This day, I decided I was going to actually pray for real. I closed my eyes really tightly, and suddenly I saw everything in the room as though my eyes were open. I was caught up in a vision.

I had never had a vision before, so I was in disbelief at first. How could my eyes be closed, but I was still seeing? As I surveyed the room it was as though I was floating through the room. I could see everyone praying but they all seemed to be frozen in the position they were in when they'd first started to pray.

As I was watching the people, suddenly I saw Him. It's difficult to express in words how I saw Him, but I had a sense of "knowing" that I was seeing Him. It's like my mind would piece together parts of the Holy Spirit, and though I couldn't fully see Him, parts of Him were being placed in my mind and reproduced in front of me. He was hovering about a foot off of the ground and He had no feet. The bottom of Him looked the same as the bottom of garments men would wear in biblical times.

The color of His garment-like body was like a beige. After I knew I was seeing parts of the Holy Spirit, He began to deliver people. The first person He delivered was a man. The Holy Spirit hovered over to the man, who seemed to be frozen. Although the Holy Spirit didn't have actual arms, the sense of knowing that I had while in this vision caused me to know that He somehow did. He placed this hand on the man's chest and it went through the man's chest. He grabbed a dark shadowy figure and slammed it against the wall with so much force that when the figure hit the wall, it disintegrated like black sand.

He then started going to everyone, one by one, at a speed not known to man. He would appear then disappear, grabbing things that were inside of people and slamming them against the walls. One by one, the shadowy figures would blow up into little tiny particles and then vanish.

I would hear the sound of them slamming against the walls, one after another. With my eyes shut I was trying to follow the Holy Spirit as He destroyed the demonic entities that were in people. Without warning, the Holy Spirit stopped and looked at me. I knew He had a face, but there was no face to look at. There were just His eyes, which were red like the blood of Jesus.

Immediately after He looked at me, I took my arms and covered my face in fear. Then the Holy Spirit looked up, and I looked up too. I found myself looking above the house we were in. The stars looked like spirits that were frozen.

In an instant, I was warped back into the house. I heard the pastor say, “amen” and everyone opened their eyes. Everyone took their chairs and made a u-shape around him. The pastor’s table and chair were brought to the top of the u-shape, and I quickly ran up to him and told him what I saw. He looked at me and he said that what I had seen was the Holy Spirit delivering people.

Jesus once spoke about how it was by the Spirit of God that He was casting out devils. He declared that it was an indication that the Kingdom of God had come. “But if I expel demons by the Spirit of God, then the kingdom of God has come upon you!” (Matthew 12:28 LEB).

When demons are being expelled from people’s souls, the kingdom of God is advancing! What a powerful passage! Additionally, when we look at all of Jesus' ministry, we can conclude without a shadow of doubt that much of it, from start to finish, had to do with expelling demons.

In Luke, Jesus describes His ministry by quoting what Isaiah had written about Him. In this passage, we read about how Jesus went up to the synagogue to read passages from the Old Testament. On this particular day, He opened the book of Isaiah and read,

"The Spirit of the Lord is upon me,
  because he has anointed me
  to proclaim good news to the poor.
He has sent me to proclaim liberty to the captives
  and recovering of sight to the blind,
  to set at liberty those who are oppressed,
to proclaim the year of the Lord's favor." (Luke 4:18-19)

This passage sums up what Jesus came to do. Likewise, we've been charged to carry this mantle and fulfill this commission. As the Spirit of the Lord was upon Jesus, it is also upon us. Therefore, we must preach the good news as He did, proclaim freedom to the captives as He did, bring sight to the blind (take people out of spiritual prison) as He did, set at liberty those who are oppressed, bring deliverance, and proclaim the year of the Lord's favor (salvation), as He did!

In many churches today, however, it seems we've become satisfied with programs. So instead of walking in power, as we were destined to, we live having a form of godliness but denying its power (2 Timothy 3:5-7). As a result, many in leadership are bound by lust, hate, jealousy, envy, selfish ambition, and sensuality, just to name a few things.

In addition, many in the church don't believe they can get demonized, and for this reason, they are unnecessarily struggling. In the vision I had earlier where the Holy Spirit was delivering people, it was at a prayer meeting. However, can a believer be under demonic influence?

Before we answer this question, let's look at what the Bible says. Paul, on many occasions, addressed the influence Satan could have on believers. One particular place Paul addressed Satan's influence on believers was in his letter to the church in Ephesus.

Prayer

Lord Jesus, You said in your Word, "But very truly I tell you, it is for your good that I am going away. Unless I go away, the Advocate will not come to you; but if I go, I will send him to you" (John 16:7 NIV). According to Your Word, it was for our good that You had to go back to Heaven because this meant we were able to get the Holy Spirit. I ask, therefore, for Your Holy Spirit to come and fill my heart. Please open up the eyes of my heart so I can see clearly and open up my ears so I can hear Your Word. In Acts 1:8, You told Your disciples that they would receive power when Your Spirit fell on them, and that this power would empower them to be Your witnesses throughout the world. I ask for this baptism, God! I pray that Your Holy Spirit would descend on me and give me my own heavenly language, just like it was for the disciples in Acts 2.

> *"When the day of Pentecost came, they were all together in one place. Suddenly a sound like the blowing of a violent wind came from heaven and filled the whole house where they were sitting. They saw what seemed to be tongues of fire that separated and came to rest on each of them. All of them were filled with the Holy Spirit and began to speak in other tongues as the Spirit enabled them" (Acts 2:1-4 NIV).*

But I want more than just a heavenly language- I want a new heart and a new mind too. I want my heart to be filled with the fruit of the Spirit. Please fill me with love, joy, peace, patience, kindness, goodness, faithfulness, gentleness, and self-control. I want to know You, God, and the only way to know You is if Your Spirit reveals who You are to me. Please reveal who Father God is to me, Holy Spirit. Please reveal more of Christ to me. Please reveal Your will for my life, Holy Spirit; reveal the truth of Your Word to me! Teach me how to love God wholeheartedly and how to love people as I love myself. Please reveal my purpose to me and help to say no to sin. In Your Mighty Name I pray, AMEN!

Chapter 4 Questions

1. According to Scripture, when demons are being expelled, it's an indication that what is happening?

2. What was Jesus anointed to do?

3. Are we called to do the same things Jesus did? If so, what are those things?

Chapter 5

THIS MEANS WAR

~~~

The city of Ephesus was located in the modern village of Selcuk, which is in western Turkey. During the Roman period, Ephesus housed the temple of the Greek goddess Artemis (or Diana, as the Romans called her).

Artemis was known as the goddess of wildlife and her followers would erotically worship her. She was depicted as a woman with multiple breasts. Many believed that her design had to do with one of her purposes, which was fertility[3].

She was worshiped alongside a water spirit named Egeria. Egeria, like Diana, was viewed as a spirit that protected pregnant women[4]. In the following chapters, we will speak more about these water spirits that are known by many as *marine spirits,* or in some cultures, *sirens*.

Many today look at these statues of Artemis/Diana and think they're just made up-fictional gods that don't really mean anything. Scripturally, however, Artemis/Diana is not just a statue but a demonic principality, an evil spirit that oversaw all of Ephesus. In Deuteronomy, Moses said this to Israelites who were worshiping false gods in the form of idols:
~~~

> "They stirred him to jealousy with strange gods; with abominations they provoked him to anger. They sacrificed to demons that were no gods, to gods they had never known, to new gods that had come recently, whom your fathers had never dreaded" (Deuteronomy 32:16-17).

Moses, in this passage, connected idols to demons. Similarly, Artemis/Diana was not just simply an idol but a demonic entity that controlled all of Ephesus. Those who worshiped her would become demonized, filled with demonic spirits.

To the people of Ephesus, Artemis/Diana was someone who protected them, helped women have children, and took care of the animals. They did not view her as a demon because demons rarely show up as demons. Normally a demonic spirit will come as something or someone who's helping you, good for you, or protecting you.

This idea that Artemis/Diana was a "good goddess" was not just in Ephesus, but it influenced all of Rome. People would come from all over the world to participate in the sexualized festivities held to her. The temple of Artemis was also beautiful to behold, and it is known as one of the seven wonders of the ancient world[5].

During his second missionary journey, Paul established the church in Ephesus (Acts 18:19). Christianity was not popular in Ephesus because people viewed it as a religion that threatened the existence of their goddess Artemis, who in their eyes, helped bring commerce to the town (Acts 19).

When Paul wrote his letter to the church in Ephesus, he was writing to a group of believers who were under constant persecution. The atmosphere would have been dark, filled with every sort of evil. It would have been imperative for every believer to know about Christ's authority and how they also were endowed with the same authority.

This authority, however, is not a fleshly one, but one that's spiritually oriented. Throughout the book of Ephesians, a person can see this theme of the authority being given in the heavenly realms (Ephesians 1:3, 20; 2:6; 3:10; 6:12). This term *heavenly realm* speaks of the spiritual world.

It is this world that the church in Ephesus was truly engaged in battle against, despite what they may have been seeing or experiencing in the natural realm. One of the last places the term heavenly realm in Paul's letter to the Ephesians is mentioned is the famous passage of Ephesians 6:10-18.

> "Finally, be strong in the Lord and in his mighty power. Put on the full armor of God, so that you can take your stand against the devil's schemes. For our struggle is not against flesh and blood, but against the rulers, against the authorities, against the powers of this dark world and against the spiritual forces of evil in the heavenly realms. Therefore, put on the full armor of God, so that when the day of evil comes, you may be able to stand your ground, and after you have done everything, to stand. Stand firm then, with the belt of truth buckled around your waist, with the breastplate of righteousness in place, and with your feet fitted with the readiness that comes from the gospel of peace. In addition to all this, take up the shield of faith, with which you can extinguish all the flaming arrows of the evil one. Take the helmet of salvation and the sword of the Spirit, which is the word of God. And pray in the Spirit on all occasions with all kinds of prayers and requests. With this in mind,

be alert and always keep on praying for all the Lord's people" (Ephesians 6:10-18 NIV).

Paul begins this section of Ephesians 6 by telling the believers in the church to *be strong in the Lord and in His mighty power* (Ephesians 6:10). This can be like when God spoke to Joshua after the death of Moses, saying, "Have I not commanded you? Be strong and courageous. Do not be afraid; do not be discouraged, for the Lord your God will be with you wherever you go" (Joshua 1:9 NIV).

Joshua was about to start his conquest of the promised land and he was going to face many enemies. God did not want him to forget that He alone was Joshua's strength. "No wisdom, no understanding, no counsel can avail against the Lord. The horse is made ready for the day of battle, but the victory belongs to the Lord" (Proverbs 21:30-31). Truly victory belongs to the Lord! If God is for us, who can be against us?

What the children of Israel faced in the natural, we face in the spiritual. Just like Joshua was preparing for war in the natural world, here, Paul speaks to believers to prepare for war in the supernatural world. Paul continues, and tells the church at Ephesus to put on the full armor of God (Ephesians 6:11). For what reason? So that they could stand against the devil's schemes.

> "The word 'scheme' in Greek is methodeía. This word has an interesting connotation. It is, in a way, depicting a direction, 'a way of search after something, an inquiry; a method.' Simply stated, it is a devised, evil plan bent on leading someone to destruction."[6]

Even though Paul had previously stated that believers are seated in the heavenly realms with Jesus and have spiritual authority, (Ephesians 2:6), he clearly indicates here that we must exercise it in the natural realm.

We don't fight these things as if they're fleshly, natural forces, for the next thing he states is that we do not wrestle against flesh and blood (Ephesians 6:12). Rather, since we live and interact in the world, we must train our flesh to combat the spiritual forces attacking this world. These forces are known as rulers or principalities, authorities, powers of this dark world, and spiritual forces of evil in the heavenly realms.

Paul tells the church in Ephesus that although they don't wrestle against flesh and blood, they are still wrestling against these forces. In Greek, the word *wrestle* is the word *palé*, which means hand-to-hand wrestling. It was used in the Greek Olympic Games. It would be equivalent to modern-day wrestling, with the objective being to subdue your opponent[7].

Paul is indicating that the battle must be engaged in. There are no spectators when it comes to battling demonic influence; everyone is called to wrestle and subdue the enemy through the power of God. The enemy we wrestle is described by Paul as "rulers or principalities, authorities, powers of this dark world, and spiritual forces of evil in the heavenly realms "(v.12).

Who is Paul talking about when he states *rulers or principalities, authorities, powers of this dark world, and spiritual forces of evil in the heavenly realms*? If we follow the progression of the verse correctly, it cannot be human beings, for it would contradict the prior statement that we don't wrestle against flesh and blood (v. 12). Clearly, these are evil spiritual entities we're in battle against.

Prayer

Jesus, I ask today that You would open the eyes of my heart so I can see the spiritual world. I'm reminded of when Elisha prayed for his servant to see spiritually and his eyes were open. Will you open my eyes like You opened Elisha's servant's eyes? (2 Kings 6:17-20) I'm also asking that You would expose every scheme of the devil. I do not want to be ignorant of Satan's schemes. Your Word says,

> *"Anyone you forgive, I also forgive. And what I have forgiven—if there was anything to forgive—I have forgiven in the sight of Christ for your sake, in order that Satan might not outwit us. For we are not unaware of his schemes" (2 Corinthians 2:10-11 NIV).*

I choose to release unforgiveness today. Lord please don't let me be outwitted by the devil today! Your Word says, "...the carnal mind is enmity against God; for it is not subject to the law of God, nor indeed can be. So then, those who are in the flesh cannot please God" (Romans 8:7-8 NKJV). Lord, help me to be in the Spirit to walk in the Spirit. Any veil that would cover my eyes please remove it in Jesus' name!

Chapter 5 Questions

1. The word "scheme" in Greek is *methodeía*. What does this mean? How does the devil use his schemes to deceive us?

2. The word *wrestle* in Greek is the word *palé*. How was this word used in Roman culture? What is the Holy Spirit trying to communicate to us through the use of this word?

Chapter 6

PRINCIPALITIES

All Scripture is inspired by God, and Paul was inspired by the Spirit of God to choose the words he used to describe evil spirits and the different types we wrestle with in Ephesians 6:12. He also seems to use a hierarchical progression to describe these demonic forces that Paul is outlining. Consequently, to better combat these forces, understanding what type of evil being you're wrestling is important.

The first on the list that Paul writes about are *rulers or principalities*. The Greek word used by Paul that means rulers or principalities is the word ἀρχὰς (arché, pronounced ar-khay') which is defined as "magisterial or kingly; something that has the priority because it's 'ahead of the rest'."[8]

Principalities, according to this description, are the strongest of the evil spirits. They are second only to Satan, who is known as "the prince of the air" (Ephesians 2:2), a murderer, and the father of lies (John 8:44). The most vivid place in the Bible where we can see principalities in operation is in the book of Daniel.

Daniel, one of the many Israelites who was taken into Babylon by king Nebuchadnezzar, had many encounters with the spiritual realm. During one of his fasts (which we've all come to know as the Daniel fast), Daniel experienced a visitation from the angel Gabriel. His whole body went into some sort of paralysis and he had no strength in him at all (Daniel 10:7-9).

Gabriel touched Daniel, who was frozen on the ground, and helped him up (v.v 10-11). Gabriel then mentioned his battle with the prince of the kingdom of Persia.

> "The prince of the kingdom of Persia withstood me twenty-one days, but Michael, one of the chief princes, came to help me, for I was left there with the kings of Persia," (Daniel 10:13).

Note that Gabriel says the being *withstood him for twenty-one days*. If this were a mere man, could he have withstood an angel like that? And let's not forget that this was no ordinary angel either. This was Gabriel, the same angel who made Zachariah mute in the book of Luke. Gabriel stands in the presence of God.

> And the angel answered him, "I am Gabriel. I stand in the presence of God, and I was sent to speak to you and to bring you this good news. And behold, you will be silent and unable to speak until the day that these things take place, because you did not believe my words, which will be fulfilled in their time" (Luke 1:19-20).

There is no way a man could withstand an angel for twenty-one days to the point where an even stronger angel had to come and deliver Gabriel. This is clearly an evil force in the heavenlies.

The word *prince* in Daniel 10:13 correlates with the word *principalities*, not with a typical earthly prince. In Hebrew, the word for prince is וְשַׂר *vesar*, which means chief captain, ruler, commander or governor[9]. Gabriel also told Daniel what region that prince was over, which was the kingdom of Persia. This region that the Persian empire encompassed was around three million square miles, spanning the continents of Asia, Africa, and Europe[10] .

This one prince that Gabriel encountered had influence and control over many territories and leaders. This would be what many also call a territorial spirit. These vile entities reign over kings, queens, presidents, prime ministers, and governors.

The devil knows that if he controls the leaders of a nation, he can dictate the direction that nation goes. The prince mentioned in Daniel 10 can be viewed dualistically. In the natural realm, it's a Persian ruler who is a host for the real power, which is a demonic principality that controls that region. This is similar to Ezekiel 28:12-19, where Satan is depicted in connection to the King of Tyre, or in Isaiah 14:12-20, where he is linked to the King of Babylon.

So how do we combat something that is able to withstand an angel like Gabriel? I believe we must do what Daniel did. We must fast and pray until we receive the breakthrough. Gabriel told Daniel that from the very first day he had humbled himself and sought out God, the answer was already sent (v.12).

Likewise, it's vital for every believer to understand the difference between Daniel's time and now. Daniel, who was a powerful righteous man of God (Ezekiel 14:14) did not possess the same authority we do. Christ had not yet died, and the Holy Spirit had not yet been given.

Thus, if Daniel's fasting and prayers were able to influence the battle in the heavenly realms, what can our prayers do for our region? Every believer should engage in this fight against the spiritual rulers over our nations, especially since our king is the King of Kings. Every believer should pray that people get disconnected from the influences of principalities and that the principalities would be pulled down and placed under our feet!

Another demonic principality that the children of Israel dealt with constantly was Baal, who was known as the prince, lord of the earth, god of fertility, and the lord of the dew and rain[11]. 1 Kings 18 depicts a major showdown that took place between Baal and Elijah, the prophet of God.

God used Elijah to show the children of Israel that Baal was an imposter. Elijah had the prophets of Baal call on him to bring down fire on an altar on top of Mount Carmel, and after they cried to Baal most of the day and cut themselves for him in hopes he would hear them, nothing happened. "It happened as noon passed, they raged until the time of the evening offering, but there was no voice, there was no answer, and no one paid attention" (1 Kings 18:29 LEB).

Then it was Elijah's turn. He first called all the children of Israel near him, which already showed the difference between the Baal who was far off and God who was wanting them near. Elijah then repaired the altar of the Lord that had been destroyed, reestablishing relationship with God and giving Him access to earth by creating a portal suitable for Him (1 Kings 18:30).

Since God gave man dominion here on earth (Genesis 1:26), He allows us to invite Him into situations. This is one of the reasons God would have the children of Israel build an altar- it was an invitation, like a person would send through the mail when they invited someone to a get-together. The stones were imperfect, and no tool was to be used on them (Exodus 20:22-26) because the altar symbolized the people. God wanted them to come as they were to be changed by Him (Romans 12:1; 1 Peter 2:3-5).

When Elijah took the stones to build the altar, Scripture emphasizes that the stones were symbolic of the twelve tribes, meaning each one represented the nation of Israel.

> "Elijah took twelve stones according to the number of the tribes of the sons of Jacob, to whom the word of God came, saying, "Israel shall be your name." With them, he built an altar in the name of Yahweh, and he made a trench which would have held about two seahs of seed, all around the altar" (1 Kings 18:31-32 LEB).

After building the altar, Elijah built a trench all around the altar and had them pour water on the altar three times till it was completely drenched. The trench was overflowing with water, possibly so that no one would think it was a trick. Then Elijah called on the God of Israel without cutting himself or dancing or screaming for hours, and God answered him by bringing fire down from the heavens and consuming the entire altar (1 Kings 18:36-39). There's a major difference between Baal, who required human blood to be shed, and the Lord, who only desired their hearts to be turned back to Him.

When I used to read this passage, I truly believed that it was at this moment that Elijah defeated Baal with God's help. But looking more closely at the entire text, I've realized that Baal was defeated prior to this event.

Baal was known as the god of rain, dew, and thunder, and those who worshiped him believed he was in charge of the skies. In 1 Kings 17, Elijah prayed that it would not rain and that there would be no dew on the land and God answered his prayer.

> "Elijah the Tishbite from Tishbe of Gilead said to Ahab, "As Yahweh lives, the God of Israel before whom I stand, there shall surely not be dew nor rain these years except by my command" (1 Kings 17:1 LEB).

Why did he pray this prayer? I believe it's in part because the people were looking to Baal as the one who supplied rain and the dew on the earth. Elijah's prayer was a direct attack against Baal, who was the principality over that region. Baal's operations were shut down after Elijah prayed; he was disarmed and rendered powerless.

This means the showdown against the prophets of Baal was already won before it ever started. Elijah overcame through prayer before he even reached Mount Carmel!

How is this applicable for us today? This story is reiterated in the book of James, where it's used to teach us how to apply it to our lives today. James says,

> "Therefore, confess your sins to one another and pray for one another, that you may be healed. The prayer of a righteous person has great power as it is working. Elijah was a man with a nature like ours, and he prayed fervently that it might not rain, and for three years and six months it did not rain on the earth. Then he prayed again, and heaven gave rain, and the earth bore its fruit" (James 5:16-18).

James begins this verse by saying that if someone is sick, they should confess their sins to another person and get prayed for so they can be healed. This is one of the greatest examples of deliverance. As the person confesses their sin, they are closing any door that they may have opened through the sins they've committed. As they get prayed for, the infirmity has to leave.

James then begins to talk about the power of prayer coming from someone in right standing with God. He states that when a righteous person actively, wholeheartedly, and fervently prays, it produces results (James 5:16 KJV). Next he begins talking about Elijah, who prayed in this manner and got the results he was seeking.

When James referenced Elijah's prayer, he made sure that the people reading his letter understood that Elijah was a man like them. Many esteemed Elijah because he had been taken to heaven by God without dying. Thus, James was trying to combat the lie that only someone of Elijah's stature could see God move in that magnitude.

What great news for us today! If God, through Elijah's prayers, could shut down the powers of Baal, withhold rain for three and a half years, and break the drought, what about us who are living under the new covenant?

The application is simple: as Christians, we should pray boldly (Hebrews 4:16). Instead of fearing that the climate is changing, we should pray against negative climate change. Our prayer life should be proactive instead of reactive. We don't need to wait for the enemy to attack us first. The fight must be brought to the enemy.

The story of Gideon is a good example of this practice. After Gideon had an encounter with the angel of the Lord, who is believed by many scholars to have been an appearance of the pre-incarnate Christ (a Christophany), Gideon was commanded by the Lord:

> "…take the bull of the cattle that belongs to your father, and a second bull seven years old, and pull down the altar of Baal that belongs to your father, and cut down the Asherah that is beside it; and build an altar to Yahweh your God on the top of this stronghold in the proper arrangement, and take a second bull and offer it as a burnt offering with the wood of the Asherah that you will cut down" (Judges 6:25-26 LEB).

Why did God have Gideon destroy the altar and cut down the idolatrous Asherah pole? Because there were demonic entities attached to the altar of Baal and the Asherah pole. Asherah is a demonic spirit connected to the water- a marine spirit. Some people referred to her as "she who walks on the sea."[12] Marine spirits are responsible for a lot of sexually immoral behaviors we see today.

The altar and the Asherah pole allowed the devil to have access and influence in that region. Altars are portals, and depending on who the altar is for, either God will have access in that area or the devil. Notice how God gives Gideon specific instructions on how to build the altar and where to put it and what to sacrifice on the altar. God told Gideon to,

> "…build an altar to the Lord your God on the top of the stronghold here, with stones laid in due order. Then take the second bull and offer it as a burnt offering with the wood of the Asherah that you shall cut down" (Judges 6:26).

Why did God have Gideon build the altar on the stronghold in a specific fashion, and then offer the seven-year-old bull as a burnt offering with the wood of the Asherah pole he had cut down?

To answer this question, we must know what a stronghold is, how God instructed the children of Israel to build altars, why the age of what's being offered as a burnt offering mattered, and why Asherah poles had to be cut down.

First of all, what is a stronghold? A stronghold is a well-fortified place, a place of defense, where a group of people would bunker to defend their territory and assets. In the natural realm, there are good strongholds and bad strongholds. Likewise, in the spirit realm, there are good strongholds and evil strongholds.

In 2 Corinthians 10:3-5, Paul states,

> "For though we walk in the flesh, we are not waging war according to the flesh. For the weapons of our warfare are not of the flesh but have divine power to destroy strongholds. We destroy arguments and every lofty opinion raised against the knowledge of God and take every thought captive to obey Christ".

The stronghold Paul is referring to is demonic, and it's designed by Satan and his demons to keep people in spiritual captivity. Examples of this kind of stronghold could be evil thoughts, lust, bitterness, deception, selfishness, self-righteousness, etc. Really, any sinful behavior can become a stronghold if not dealt with through repentance. This type of stronghold is designed by demonic entities to keep truth out and lies in.

But there is also a good kind of stronghold. In Psalm 27:1, David calls God “the stronghold of [his] life”. In this passage David uses the word stronghold in a positive way. He is essentially saying that God is his place of safety. Therefore, if satanic strongholds keep lies in and truth out, then the reverse would be true about a godly stronghold. It keeps lies out and truth in.

Gideon was instructed to build an altar on the enemy’s fortress to subdue the demonic powers over that region. By building an altar on top of the stronghold, Gideon destroyed the command post of the demonic spirits. The altar that was built had to be done in a very specific way. God's altars represented His people, so they were made of dirt and unhewn stones (Exodus 20:24-25). God wants us to come as we are and allow His fire to consume and mold us.

An altar created from hewn stones, in God’s eyes, represents man’s workmanship instead of God’s creation. Man can easily feel as though it was their altar presentation that caused God to come. It’s another depiction of the gospel, which can be symbolized by the unhewn stones, versus man’s works, which would be hewn stones.

God instructed Gideon to sacrifice the bull that was seven years old. Seven is a significant number in the Bible. Every seventh year, the Israelites were commanded by God to release servants, forgive debt, and let the land rest.

Seven is also the number associated the most with God (Genesis 2:1; Isaiah 11:2; Revelation 1:4-5, 3:1, 4:5, 5:6). It is therefore no coincidence that the bull was seven years old. This could have been symbolically hinting at the seventh sabbatical year, which would have been a year of freedom and rest.

God wanted a pure sacrifice, and the seven-year-old bull represented this because it was young and innocent. You can see a glimpse of Calvary in this story. Jesus, who is the pure and innocent sacrificial lamb who died for us on a cross that symbolized the curses of sin, opened the way so we could enter into God's sabbatical rest for eternity.

We have already established earlier that the Asherah poles were idols to Asherah, the marine goddess. Throughout Scripture, God told the children of Israel to completely destroy all the false gods in every land they conquered or even in their own land. So, cutting the Asherah pole and using it as fuel for the fire that the burnt offering was going to be lit on was a way of God having Gideon completely destroy the powers of that false god.

Although you read later on in Gideon's story about him defeating the Philistines, his war was won first in the supernatural realm on the day he destroyed Baal's altar and tore down the Asherah pole.

The spiritual victory preceded the physical one. Likewise, we must also tear apart demonic altars and get rid of items we've allowed to infiltrate our homes, our bodies, our communities, and our churches if we want to see our nation turn around. This does not mean we must physically tear down the statues in our communities; rather, we must engage against the entities behind them and pull down the demonic principalities that are connected to them.

Prayer

(Consider fasting, if you feel led to by the Holy Spirit)

Lord, Your Word says, "In the beginning God created the heavens and the earth" (Genesis 1:1 NIV). The earth and everything in it belongs to You. I declare Psalm 24:

> *"The earth is the Lord's, and everything in it, the world, and all who live in it; for he founded it on the seas and established it on the waters. Who may ascend the mountain of the Lord? Who may stand in his holy place? The one who has clean hands and a pure heart, who does not trust in an idol or swear by a false god. They will receive blessing from the Lord and vindication from God their Savior. Such is the generation of those who seek him, who seek your face, God of Jacob. Lift up your heads, you gates; be lifted up, you ancient doors, that the King of glory may come in. Who is this King of glory? The Lord strong and mighty, the Lord mighty in battle. Lift up your heads, you gates; lift them up, you ancient doors, that the King of glory may come in. Who is he, this King of glory? The Lord Almighty— he is the King of glory" (Psalms 24:1-10 NIV).*

The earth is Yours, God; it's all Yours. I repent for my sins and I'm asking You to forgive me and purify my heart. Lord, I'm also asking that You would vindicate me. Principalities have come and robbed me, oppressed me, and delayed my purpose in many ways. Please disconnect me from them in the mighty name of Jesus. O King of Glory, Lord strong in battle, please fight for my family, friends, my community, and myself. Some of these principalities have even affected the weather in my region. I ask that where there has been drought, it would rain; where there was flood, it would cease. If Elijah who was a man like me prayed and it affected the weather, surely I, too, can pray that the weather would change so that the crops could grow and the economy would prosper. In the mighty name of Jesus I pray, AMEN!

Chapter 6 Questions

1. What is the word for "principalities" in Greek and what does it mean? How is this word similar to the Hebrew word *vesar?*

2. Why does the author believe that Gabriel is referring to a spiritual being in Daniel 10:13?

3. How do we combat principalities? What's the difference between Daniel's encounter with principalities living under the Old Covenant and our engagement with them living under the New Covenant?

Chapter 7

THE AUTHORITIES

Paul also mentions *authorities or powers.* Authorities is the word exousia (ἐξουσίας), which is defined as "force, capacity, freedom, or mastery". It refers to the leading and more powerful among the created beings that are superior to mankind.[13]

Authorities make sure that the evil produced by the principalities is accomplished. Demonic spirits are liars and are only intent on producing death. These authorities subjugate people, use legal rights given by people to control them, overpower those who are not under the protection of Jesus Christ, force their will upon human beings, and attempt to enslave the human race.

These beings utilize different platforms and social networks to accomplish their schemes. Authorities oversee every evil propaganda. They spread immorality through ungodly laws and push evil "mores"- norms, actions, customs in a society that are deemed acceptable by the society or social groups. Paul said to Timothy,

> "Now the Spirit expressly says that in latter times some will depart from the faith by devoting themselves to deceitful spirits and teachings of demons, through the insincerity of liars whose consciences are seared,

who forbid marriage and require abstinence from foods that God created to be received with thanksgiving by those who believe and know the truth." (1 Timothy 4:1-3).

These teachings or doctrines are influenced by principalities and authorities. They use people who have no conviction, are liars, and are immature in the Lord to alter the gospel of freedom in the church. In the world, they change the times and laws in society. The gospel is altered in the church by promoting customs of men as though they were the commandments of God.

As these customs of man are promoted, faith is slowly pushed out of the church and man's religion takes center stage. It's imperative, therefore, for believers to understand the difference between faith and man's religion. The word *faith* in Greek is *pistis* and it means "divine persuasive trust". Faith persuades.

Man's religion, on the other hand, is compulsive. It torments you into submission and forces an individual to obey out of fear of punishment. This is why God does not like it when we give out of compulsiveness (2 Corinthians 9:7) rather than cheerfulness.

Religion consists of demonically inspired wisdom, and we can see this in the Word when Peter rebuked Jesus when He said He was going to suffer by the hands of the elders and chief priests and die (Matthew 16:21).

"And Peter took him aside and began to rebuke him, saying, "Far be it from you, Lord! This shall never happen to you." But he turned and said to Peter, "Get behind me, Satan! You are a hindrance to me. For you are

> not setting your mind on the things of God, but on the things of man'" (Matthew 16:22-23).

Notice how a statement that seems wise and full of love can actually be directly from Satan. This was just a simple and seemingly loving rebuke, yet Jesus deemed it satanic. What about what we say and do on a regular basis! How much of it is poisoned by Satan even though we are in the very presence of Jesus!

Man's wisdom can be demonic yet sound godly. James warns us about this type of wisdom when he states,

> "But if you have bitter jealousy and selfish ambition in your hearts, do not boast and be false to the truth. This is not the wisdom that comes down from above, but is earthly, unspiritual, demonic. For where jealousy and selfish ambition exist, there will be disorder and every vile practice" (James 3:14-16).

When you view this passage in light of what Peter said to Jesus, you can conclude that Peter's rebuke was selfish. It had to do with man's desires instead of Gods will; therefore, it was demonic.

Principalities and authorities also influence the world by changing the times and laws. Daniel spoke about this when he was writing about the end times and what the antichrist, a man under the influence of Satan, would do.

> "He shall speak words against the Most High, and shall wear out the saints of the Most High, and shall think to change the times and the law; and they shall be given into his hand for a time, times, and half a time" (Daniel 7:25).

One commentary states that the changing of times and laws involves things like granting pardons for sins, appointing fasts and feasts, and canonizing saints. Likewise, it involves "instituting new modes of worship, imposing new articles of faith, enjoining new rules of practice, and reversing at pleasure the laws of God and man"[14].

We are already seeing this influence in our world today. Marriage, which was a law set by God, has now been altered from being a union between a man and a woman to including homosexual relationships. Gender, which has always solely been male or female, can now be defined as fluid.

A woman and a man are no longer defined by their God-given purposes but instead are defined by whatever society deems them to be. Emotions and thoughts are no longer filtered by truth, but by the mores of the day. All these things are a result of principalities and authorities operating amongst us, changing times, laws, customs, and traditions.

But Jesus disarmed them and nailed every legal indebtedness to the cross. Paul wrote about this triumphant victory when he stated,

> "And you, who were dead in your trespasses and the uncircumcision of your flesh, God made alive together with him, having forgiven us all our trespasses, by canceling the record of debt that stood against us with its legal demands. This he set aside, nailing it to the cross. He disarmed the rulers and authorities and put them to open shame, by triumphing over them in him. Therefore let no one pass judgment on you in questions of food and drink, or with regard to a festival or a new moon or a Sabbath. These are a shadow of the things to come, but the substance belongs to

> Christ. Let no one disqualify you, insisting on asceticism and worship of angels, going on in detail about visions, puffed up without reason by his sensuous mind, and not holding fast to the Head, from whom the whole body, nourished and knit together through its joints and ligaments, grows with a growth that is from God. If with Christ you died to the elemental spirits of the world, why, as if you were still alive in the world, do you submit to regulations— "Do not handle, Do not taste, Do not touch" (referring to things that all perish as they are used)—according to human precepts and teachings? These have indeed an appearance of wisdom in promoting self-made religion and asceticism and severity to the body, but they are of no value in stopping the indulgence of the flesh" (Colossians 2:13-23).

In this passage Paul is first reminding the church at Colossae that they used to walk as the world walks now, dead in their trespasses. But God brought them to life, nailed all their sins upon the cross, and canceled every legal debt they owed. This in no way means we aren't obligated to ask for forgiveness, as some assume. If this was true, most of the Bible would be irrelevant because repentance is a key component of salvation (Acts 2:38).

What it does mean is that the full forgiveness for our wrongdoing has been covered and we just have to admit, submit, and resist. We have to admit that we are sinners, and when we sin, we must admit that we sin.

> "If we say we have no sin, we deceive ourselves, and the truth is not in us. If we confess our sins, he is faithful and just to forgive us our sins and to cleanse us from all unrighteousness. If we say we have not sinned, we make him a liar, and his word is not in us" (1 John 1:8-10).

We also need to submit to God by surrendering areas of pain and sin to Him, as well as resisting the devil so he'll flee.

What does it mean to *submit* to God? The word submit in Greek is the word *hupotassó* which means to place under, subject or obey[15]. To be someone's subject is to become a slave to that person. Paul wrote to the Roman church saying that while we were once slaves of sin, we have now become "slaves of righteousness" (Romans 6:17-18).

A slave must obey His master no matter what, and our master is Jesus Christ. We must know we are loved by Jesus as sons and daughters and submit as though we are His slaves. This type of slavery, however, is not one based on worthlessness, but rather on complete devotion.

Christ wants us to become completely obedient to His will. In other words, we are required by God to not just listen to His Word but to do what it says (James 1:22-25). As we do what His Word says, there is a blessing that comes, and we are now empowered to resist.

The Greek word for resist is *anthistémi* (anth-is'-tay-mee). This word biblically means to stand firm in something and against what may be opposing you. This firm stance should be done both publicly and consciously, and we must refuse to be moved from the foundational truth of God's Word[16].
The devil does not stay away from a believer forever, for even when he left Jesus, he waited for an opportune time to return (Luke 4:13).

Since the devil will wait for an opportune time to return, resisting him must be continual. By resisting, we are committing to have a genuine relationship with God, His Word, and His church. Jesus said that if we abide in

His Word, we would know the truth, and the truth would set us free (John 8:32). We must first believe in Him, for He spoke to Jews who believed in Him. Then we abide in His Word, proving we are His disciples. After this we will know the truth, and the truth will set us free!

Continuing on, Paul mentions rulers and authorities. The rulers and authorities that Paul mentions are spiritual demonic forces. Jesus disarmed them, taking their armor as one who conquers an enemy would do[17]. They did not understand, according to 1 Corinthians 2:8, that they were going to be conquered through the death of Christ. If they had, they would never have crucified Him.

He put them to open shame by publicly being crucified and triumphed over them as He rose again from the dead! It's what Jesus did on the cross that empowered us and made us more than conquerors. As Paul wrote in Romans 8, nothing can separate us from the love God has for us through Jesus.

Nothing outside of ourselves can ever separate us from the love of God. Therefore, we need not worry about regulatory things as means of our salvation. Paul says in Colossians 2 that the substance is Christ. Our obligation is no longer to customs that were mere shadows of Jesus. This can lead us to be deceived by rulers and authorities who will try to enslave us by accusing us of not being able to fulfill all the law's demands.

Jesus fulfilled the law and trusting Him will help a person walk in freedom. Unfortunately, some take this passage and make it a license for ignorance. They think they can touch or eat whatever they want, but this is not the case. There are certainly things, if we touch or eat, that can hinder our walk with the Lord, especially if we have unrepentant hearts.

"Consider the people of Israel: are not those who eat the sacrifices participants in the altar? What do I imply then? That food offered to idols is anything, or that an idol is anything? No, I imply that what pagans sacrifice they offer to demons and not to God. I do not want you to be participants with demons. You cannot drink the cup of the Lord and the cup of demons. You cannot partake of the table of the Lord and the table of demons. Shall we provoke the Lord to jealousy? Are we stronger than he? (1 Corinthians 10:18-22)."

Therefore, it is important that whatever we eat, drink, buy, or are even gifted with should be covered in prayer. As the Word of God says, "everything God created is good, and nothing is to be rejected if it is received with thanksgiving, because it is consecrated by the word of God and prayer" (1 Timothy 4:4-5 NIV).

The passage is not saying everything in this world man creates is good, but rather everything *God* has created is good. People can invent evil things (Romans 1:30). We should never think that praying over something evil, like a pornographic magazine, will redeem it. No amount of prayer can redeem it.

If the Holy Spirit says to not even touch something, then don't do it. Sometimes things are so corrupted by the flesh that the Lord will tell us to not be even associated with them. As Jude wrote, "save others by snatching them out of the fire; to others show mercy with fear, hating even the garment stained by the flesh" (Jude 1:23).

Demonic principalities and authorities want to make us overly righteous so that we follow the law instead of Christ. This will cause us to fall away from grace (Galatians 5:4). They may also try to cause us to walk in sin so that it leads us to death (Romans 6:23). Solomon wrote about the temptations of these seemingly two polarizing habits that are both a trap.

> "In my vain life I have seen everything. There is a righteous man who perishes in his righteousness, and there is a wicked man who prolongs his life in his evildoing. Be not overly righteous, and do not make yourself too wise. Why should you destroy yourself? Be not overly wicked, neither be a fool. Why should you die before your time? It is good that you should take hold of this, and from that withhold not your hand, for the one who fears God shall come out from both of them" (Ecclesiastes 7:15-18).

Self-righteousness is a trap and will lead a person on a path of self-destruction. On the other hand, though, wicked people may attempt to live longer through doing evil. On the contrary, they're actually making themselves susceptible to dying before their time. The only way to come out of both of these traps is to fear (respect, honor, revere, love) God completely.

Prayer

Lord, I need your help. I have been swayed by the world because I have followed the social mores (customs) of the world. I have allowed demonic authorities to influence my thought processes and actions. Your Word says,

> *"Do not love the world or anything in the world. If anyone loves the world, love for the Father is not in them. For everything in the world—the lust of the flesh, the lust of the eyes, and the pride of life—comes not from the Father but from the world. The world and its desires pass away, but whoever does the will of God lives forever" (1 John 2:15-17 NIV).*

Forgive me for loving worldly things. I have fallen prey to the lust of the flesh, the lust of the eyes, and the pride of life. Please deliver me from these things!

Social media, books, TV shows, and movies have shaped my belief system. Please forgive me and break this stronghold off of me! At times, I have believed that through my righteousness I can rescue myself from sin. Please forgive me for being overly righteous. Forgive me for thinking I need to regulate everyone and force my convictions on them. Forgive me for also living a sinful life. For compromising the Word of God and not standing on the truth. You declared that even Heaven and earth would pass away, but Your words would not pass away (Matthew 24:35). I agree that Your Word is a lamp to my feet and a light to my path (Psalm 119:105). Let Your Word break every religious chain and burn away every wicked desire that has been keeping me bound. For you told Jeremiah that Your Word is like fire, "and like a hammer that breaks the rock in pieces" (Jeremiah 23:29). Thank you, Lord for all that you have done! Amen!

Chapter 7 Questions

1. What are the *authorities?*

2. How do authorities operate?

3. What are the two things' authorities are seeking to do and how do they accomplish it?

4. How do authorities use religion to advance their evil agenda?

Chapter 8

COSMIC POWERS OVER THIS PRESENT DARKNESS

~~~

Paul next mentions *the cosmic powers over this present darkness.* Wicked spirits must be viewed militarily-they have rank and order. Demonic spirits are militant.

We know this based on the interaction Jesus had with the demoniacs. Jesus told his disciples that they should go to the other side of the Sea of Galilee to the Gentile country of the Gerasenes. While they were traveling, a storm arose out of nowhere while Jesus stayed asleep in the boat.

This story is similar to that of Jonah, who went to Tarshish in a boat in an attempt to run away from God. God sent a storm, but Jonah was asleep (Jonah 1:5). While Jonah was running away from the will of God, however, Jesus was in the will of God.

Both storms are arguably supernatural. The storm that Jonah was in was caused by God (Jonah 1:4), while the storm Jesus was in may have been caused by demonic principalities over that region. Some commentaries say Jesus' storm was demonically influenced because He had to rebuke it.
~~~

The Greek word for *rebuke* is *epetimēsen,* which means to reprimand or strongly admonish[18]. Jesus used this same word many times when He was casting out devils. One commentary states,

> "Jesus didn't merely quiet the wind and the sea; He rebuked the winds and the sea. This, along with the disciple's great fear, and what Jesus would confront at their destination, gives the sense that Satan had a significant hand in this storm"[19].

As Jesus crossed the Sea of Galilee into this region, He headed toward the territory of the Greco-Roman gods[20]- the land of the Gerasenes. The people in this territory held Hellenistic beliefs and worshipped Roman and Greek gods. These false gods, according to Deuteronomy 32:16-17, were really evil spirits in disguise.

These Greco-Roman gods were the regional evil spirits causing the thunderstorm and stirring up the sea, and in rebuking the storm, Jesus was really rebuking them. This is possibly why the spirits were allowed to go into the pigs who were used sacrificially for the worship of Zeus or other Greco-Roman deities, as Antiochus Epiphanes did during the Maccabean revolt[21].

After He rebuked the storm (Luke 8:22-25), He and His disciples reached the country of the Gerasenes. Immediately, Jesus was met with a man who was completely influenced by malevolent spirits.

After attempting to cast these spirits out, Jesus asked, "What is your name?" "Legion," he replied, for he was filled with many demons (Luke 8:30 NLT). The word *legion* in the Roman period was a military word. A Roman legion typically had 4,000 to 6,000 troops and they were ordered by rank.

The Roman army was separated up into legions. Each legion was composed of 10 cohorts, each containing 480 men. The first cohort would have had double that number. This means there was around 5,280 men (legionaries) in one legion.

Each cohort was subdivided into six centuries of 80 men that the centurion controlled. These groups were divided into smaller groups with different jobs that they had to perform. Lastly, there were the horsemen, calvary, and other foot soldiers, each specializing in different things[22].

Jesus' divine nature assures us that He knew the demoniac's name. Thus, in asking this question, Jesus revealed to us how evil spirits operate. They are militant, taking commands and executing missions. You can get a good picture of how they function by looking at how Roman legions operated[23].

A legion had 4,000 to 6,000 soldiers and was led by the legatus, or legate. Legates had to be at least 30 years old and were senators who had already been praetors in Rome. A praetor was a Roman who ranked below a consul and had mainly judicial functions[24].

A praetor was under the consul, who commanded the army and was a head of state. They commanded the army, oversaw the Senate, executed decrees, and represented the state in foreign affairs[25]. After consuls retired, they could then become governors of provinces and they received unlimited powers. Lastly, above all governors in Rome was Ceasar.

When you look at the list of evil spiritual entities that Paul mentions, each of these reflects, in a way, the Roman government. Ceasar would be likened to Satan; the governors would be principalities; consuls could possibly represent *authorities*. The *cosmic powers of this present darkness* may be comparable to the praetors who oversaw the civil laws and entertainment for the citizens.

Legates who led the legions could be compared to spiritual forces of evil. Lastly, demons could represent centuries, calvary, horsemen, and specialists in the Roman army.

While demonic hierarchy doesn't *exactly* reflect how the demonic kingdom operates, it's meant to help you understand that there's a demonic kingdom (Matthew 12:26) with its own governing system, and in this kingdom, evil spirits have ranks[26]. Why would this be valuable for a believer? Because some higher-ranking demonic entities may require a different spiritual method to take them out of an individual.

For instance, when the disciples could not cast out the demon in a young boy, Jesus had to come and cast it out for them. The disciples following this asked Jesus why they could not cast out the demon and Jesus said, "This kind cannot be driven out by anything but prayer"' (Mark 9:29).

Notice how Jesus says *this kind*. There are different kinds of demonic spirits, and if this kind cannot be cast out except through prayer, then when we're dealing with demonic forces, it's important to know what kind we are dealing with, so we know how to cast them out. Not every wicked spirit that we face is the same in power or has the same assignment as another one. They may have the same goal-to steal, kill, and destroy (John 10:10)- but how they accomplish that goal varies from demonic entity to demonic entity.

Jesus then describes what an unclean spirit does after it leaves a person. It comes back to that person, finds that things have been "swept…and put in order", and goes and gathers other demons stronger than itself.

> "When the unclean spirit has gone out of a person, it passes through waterless places seeking rest, but finds none. Then it says, 'I will return to my house from which I came.' And when it comes, it finds the house empty, swept, and put in order. Then it goes and brings with it seven other spirits more evil than itself, and they enter and dwell there, and the last state of that person is worse than the first. So also will it be with this evil generation" (Matthew 12:43-45).

First and foremost, Jesus is explaining that an unclean spirit can travel. Secondly, it needs to rest, meaning evil spirits get tired. Third, a human being is considered to be a house for an unclean spirit. Next, Jesus shows that evil spirits can speak. Lastly, when it finds the place swept and clean, it gets seven other evil spirits stronger than itself. This shows that unclean spirits are strategic, work together to accomplish goals, and vary in degrees of evil power.

On Paul's list of demonic forces, cosmic powers over this present darkness are third on the hierarchy. The word *cosmic* in Greek is *kosmokratór* (kos-mok-rat'-ore) and it refers to a ruler of the world, a demonic power, that controls the sublunary world[27].

The term *sublunary* is defined as something beneath the moon that's connected to earth. Kosmokratór can further be broken up into the words *kosmos* and *krateó*. Kosmos refers to something that is well-arranged and in unison. Just as Roman soldiers operated in harmony, these demonic beings stay united and are ready to take orders from Satan, the principalities, and authorities[28]. Wicked spirits can be agents of chaos, but they are not chaotic in their operations.

Krateó on the other hand, is defined as ruling, placing under one's grasp, or putting under control. Another way to better understand this word is to look at the different ways it's used in Scripture. It takes on many definitions, including the following:

- arrested
- attained
- clinging
- held
- hold
- hold fast
- holding back
- holding fast
- holds
- laid hold
- observe
- observing
- prevented
- retain
- retained
- seize
- seized
- take custody
- take hold
- taking
- took

- took hold[29]

Based on these definitions, you can conclude that "cosmic powers over this present darkness" are orderly evil beings who work to control and arrest individuals under the legal system created by the authorities. There is no winning with the devil. Not only do they change the laws, but they also take people into custody to live by these laws while simultaneously attempting to enforce them on those who don't.

When they are not demonizing human beings or creatures, these demonic beings' dwell in the sublunary (beneath the moon and connected to the earth). The evil legality these beings have orchestrated makes it easier for them to make sin right and right wrong. People unaware of this distortion get coerced into living in darkness and thinking it's the light.

Prayer

Lord, in the book of Psalms, David said, "You train my hands for war and my fingers for battle" (Psalm 144:1). Please train my hands for war also. Strengthen me so that I may stand against the cosmic powers of this present darkness that are using immorality and sin to destroy me. I admit that I have lived a sinful life. Your Word says,

> *"What causes quarrels and what causes fights among you? Is it not this, that your passions are at war within you? You desire and do not have, so you murder. You covet and cannot obtain, so you fight and quarrel. You do not have, because you do not ask. You ask and do not receive, because you ask wrongly, to spend it on your passions. You adulterous people! Do you not know that friendship with the world is enmity with God? Therefore whoever wishes to be a friend of the world makes himself an enemy of God. Or do you suppose it is to no purpose that the Scripture says, "He yearns jealously over the spirit that he has made to dwell in us"? But he gives more grace. Therefore it says, "God opposes the proud but gives grace to the humble" (James 4:1-6).*

Lord, at times my fleshly passions are at war within me. When I yield to my fleshly passions, I quarrel with people and what I ask for comes from the wrong motives. Please deliver me from these evil passions. Help me not to be proud, for I do not want You to oppose me. I put on humility in place of pride. I submit to Your will for my life and I resist the devil. As Your Word declares: "Submit yourselves therefore to God. Resist the devil, and he will flee from you" (James 4:7). I command, therefore, every demonic spirit that came into my life because of my fleshly passions to get out now in Jesus' name (repeat until you feel a total release).

I commit myself fully to you and declare Colossians 3:

If then (I) have been raised with Christ, (I will) seek the things that are above, where Christ is, seated at the right hand of God. (I will) set (my) mind on things that are above, not on things that are on earth. For (I) died, and (my) life is hidden with Christ in God. When Christ, who is (my) life, appears, then (I) also will appear with Him in glory.

(I) put to death what is earthly in (me): sexual immorality, impurity, passion, evil desire, and covetousness, which is idolatry. On account of these, the wrath of God is coming. In these (I) too once walked, when (I was) living in them. But now (I) must put them all away: anger, wrath, malice, slander, and obscene talk from (my) mouth.

I will not lie to my brother or sister in the Lord, because I have put off (my) old self with its practices and have put on (my) new self, which is being renewed in knowledge after the image of its creator. Here there is not Greek and Jew, circumcised and uncircumcised, barbarian, Scythian, slave, free; but Christ is all, and in all. (I) put on, then, as God's chosen vessel, holy and beloved, a compassionate heart, kindness, humility, meekness, and patience, (I) choose to bear with (others), I will forgive other as Christ has forgiven me.

And above all these (I will) put on love, which binds everything together in perfect harmony. And let the peace of Christ rule in (my) heart, to which indeed (I was) called in one body. And (I will) be thankful. Let the word of Christ dwell in (me) richly, and teaching and admonishing others in all wisdom, (I will) sing psalms and hymns and spiritual songs, with thankfulness in (my) heart to God. And whatever (I) do, in word or deed, (help me to do) everything in the name of the Lord Jesus, giving thanks to God the Father through him. Amen!

Chapter 8 Questions

1. What are cosmic powers over this present darkness?

2. How do they operate?

3. Does Satan have a kingdom? If so, how does his kingdom operate?

4. Why is it important to know that demons have ranks?

5. What does kosmokratór mean?

Chapter 9

SPIRITUAL FORCES OF EVIL IN THE HEAVENLY PLACES

Last on Paul's list of malevolent spirits are *the spiritual forces of evil in the heavenly places.* These demonic forces are like the legates who led the Roman legion armies. The word *evil* in *spiritual forces of evil* is the Greek word *ponéria* (pon-ay-ree'-ah).

This word means many things, including "malicious intentions, disposed to construe words and phrases, knavish trickery, and in a political connotation, it refers to mob rule."[30] Ponéria is also derived from the Greek word *ponos*, which means to tire down with toil, afflict, or oppress with evil[31]. Ponos is also part of a word we know and refer to as *oppression.*

In Greek, the word oppression is *kataponeó*. It means is to wear something down; to overpower something and cause it to suffer. Kataponeó can be further broken down into two words. The first one is *kata*, which refers to bringing something down from a higher place to a lower place continuously.

The second word is *ponos* which means pain, intense desire, great trouble, and labor. This word is also personified by a Greek god named Ponos, who is a demonic entity[32]. When Peter recounted how Jesus had appeared to the Gentiles, he stated that God "anointed Jesus of Nazareth with the Holy Spirit and with power. He went about doing good and healing all who were oppressed by the devil, for God was with him" (Acts 10:38).

The word *oppressed* here is the Greek word *katadynasteuomenous*. It means "to powerfully bring someone down, taking away them the higher position or blessing they should enjoy."[33]

Every demonic entity tries to oppress people in one way or another. These last mischievous spirits on Paul's list oppress the human race tyrannically. They exercise rulership over humanity, bring the human race pain, stop people's blessings, manifest unfathomable wickedness, and cause people to work purposelessly.

They bring infirmities, depression, anxiety, and various afflictions both known and unknown to men. Furthermore, these demonic entities entice men to act out in the works of the flesh that Paul mentions in Galatians.

> Now the works of the flesh are evident: sexual immorality, impurity, sensuality, idolatry, sorcery, enmity, strife, jealousy, fits of anger, rivalries, dissensions, divisions, envy, drunkenness, orgies, and things like these. I warn you, as I warned you before, that those who do such things will not inherit the kingdom of God (Galatians 5:19-21).

These works of the flesh can also be understood as doors into the soul. In Ephesians 4, Paul addressed the church in Ephesus about the importance of not opening the door to the enemy through unforgiveness.

> "Therefore, putting away lying, "Let each one of you speak truth with his neighbor," for we are members of one another. "Be angry, and do not sin": do not let the sun go down on your wrath, nor give place to the devil" (Ephesians 4:25-27 NKJV).

This passage here is not directed at unbelievers, but at believers. Paul is telling the believers not to give the devil a *topos*, or a *place*, in their lives. Some translations use the word *foothold,* like when you try to shut a door, and someone sticks their foot in it to keep it from shutting. That person's foot in the door creates enough space for him or her to make a wider opening and come in.

Any work of the flesh can give the devil a foothold. This is one of the ways different demonic spirits can enter an individual. Demonic spirits live in unclean places, which is why the demoniacs lived among the tombs (Mark 5).

But there is a more unclean place than a tomb, and that place is the human heart. That's why Jesus says nothing coming into a human heart defiles a person, but it's what comes out of them that defiles them.

> "And he said, "What comes out of a person is what defiles him. For from within, out of the heart of man, come evil thoughts, sexual immorality, theft, murder, adultery, coveting, wickedness, deceit, sensuality, envy, slander, pride, foolishness. All these evil things come from within, and they defile a person"" (Mark 7:20-23).

All of the sins Jesus mentions are open doors. True defilement is the sin within. If evil entities live in places that are unclean, then are we not provoking them to live in us when we make our hearts suitably apt for them? The doors that we open or that others have opened in our hearts are like big signs that say,

"Come and live here!" *This is why, without repentance, no man can enter the Kingdom of God.*

Thus, we can reasonably say that devil isn't the biggest problem- our hearts are. This is especially made evident through the life of Judas Iscariot. Before Satan came into Judas, Judas' heart was already defiled.

The Bible tells us that Judas was a greedy individual. One day while Jesus and his disciples were fellowshipping with Lazarus, Mary, and Martha, Mary took an expensive ointment made from pure nard and anointed Jesus' feet with her hair. Judas criticized Jesus and Mary, saying they should have sold it and given the money to the poor (John 12:1-5).

This sounded wise and godly, but he wasn't saying this because he cared about the poor, but because "he was a thief, and having charge of the moneybag he used to help himself to what was put into it" (John 12:6). Judas' heart was greedy and unclean, making it a perfect place for demonic spirits to dwell.

The Bible tells us that the love of money is a root of all kinds of evil. Because of the love of money, "some have wandered away from the faith and pierced themselves with many pangs" (1 Timothy 6:10). Notice how it says some have "wandered away" from the faith, meaning they were originally in the faith, and they opened this door that caused them to leave the faith. This is one of the main goals of the demonic spirits: to separate you from Jesus.

In Judas' case, his love for money did just that. It caused him to not only wander away from Jesus, but even to betray him. The door of greed that he opened let Satan in.

> "Then Satan entered into Judas called Iscariot, who was of the number of the twelve. He went away and conferred with the chief priests and officers how he might betray him to them. And they were glad, and agreed to give him money. So he consented and sought an opportunity to betray him to them in the absence of a crowd" (Luke 22:3-6).

Judas would eventually go on to hang himself (Acts 1:16-18). However, it's important to note that none of what took place in Judas' life just happened overnight. It all started with him giving into his flesh, thus opening the door to the enemy and coming completely under Satan's influence.

We too can open doors in our lives. James said,

> "Let no one say when he is tempted, "I am being tempted by God," for God cannot be tempted with evil, and he himself tempts no one. But each person is tempted when he is lured and enticed by his own desire. Then desire when it has conceived gives birth to sin, and sin when it is fully grown, brings forth death" (James 1:13-15).

Death, then, is the ultimate goal of these demonic entities. That's why the Bible says that the thief comes only to steal, kill, and destroy (John 10:10). This verse also states, however, that Jesus came so that we may have life more abundantly. Life is greater than death.

The spiritual forces of evil in the heavenly places entice humanity, oppress mankind, cause individuals to work purposelessly, keep people in a poverty mentality, or give people temporary riches because they know the love of money is the root of all evil. Their ultimate goal is to destroy the human race.

If we practice sinning, we become easily susceptible to their destruction. The good news is that Jesus came to free us!

> "Whoever makes a practice of sinning is of the devil, for the devil has been sinning from the beginning. The reason the Son of God appeared was to destroy the works of the devil" (1 John 3:8).

Now, the spiritual forces of evil in the heavenly places, although last on Paul's list of demonic forces in Ephesians 6:12, are not the final demonic spirits. There are other beings that the Old and New Testament calls *demons* that are different from these four categorizations of evil spirits.

Satan's fallen angels were not the only ones who sinned against God and left their proper place. The Bible speaks in Genesis 6 and other places in Scripture about other angelic beings that left heaven and came down to the earth. These fallen angels had offspring known as the Nephilim, Raphiam, Uzzim, Emim, fallen ones, or giants, whose spirits are rightfully perceived by some as demons. We will look more at these entities in the following chapters.

Prayer

"Lord, battle with those who battle with me. Fight against those who fight against me. Pick up the shield and armor. Rise up and help me. Lift up your spears, both large and small, against those who chase me. Tell me, "I will save you"' (Psalms 35:1-3 NCV).

God, you made me on purpose for a purpose. The spiritual forces of evil in the heavenly places are seeking to cause me to work purposelessly so that I can live a purposeless life. I have helped them by opening doors through sin and I have given them the right to torment me. Jesus, please forgive me, and in Your name I pray that their oppression would lift off of me! Please expose every hidden motive in my heart. Please destroy the works of the devil in my life! I do not want to live with a poverty mentality anymore. I repent of living with this mentality and ask for Your mind, Jesus! You said I have Your mind; please help me to think like you! Like Judas, there have been many times in my life I've betrayed you. Please forgive me and completely disconnect me from the spiritual forces of evil in the heavenly places. Amen!

Chapter 9 Questions

1. What are the spiritual forces of evil in the heavenly places?

2. What does the word *ponos* mean and how does the author connect it to the spiritual forces of evil in the heavenly places?

3. How do the spiritual forces of evil in the heavenly places operate?

4. What caused Judas to walk away from God?

5. How do demons come into an individual?

Chapter 10

THE SONS OF GOD

After Adam and Eve fell in Genesis 3, they went from being a part of the family of God to being separated from God. Gradually, men began to become enemies of God instead of friends of God (Genesis 6:3; Colossians 1:21; Romans 5:10). Mankind no longer had the same relationship that Adam and Eve had once had.

Then in Genesis 5, we read about a godly line that begins with one of Adam's sons, Seth, who is his spitting image. However, even this godly line could not repair the damage that was done because of sin. "When Adam sinned, sin entered the world. Adam's sin brought death, so death spread to everyone, for everyone sinned" (Romans 5:12 NLT).

This godly line that came through Seth's lineage didn't have pure genetics because they weren't sinless. Therefore, the passage in Genesis 6 about sons of God having sexual relations with the daughters of men cannot be referring to Seth's line simply because there is no difference genetically at this point between Seth's lineage and Cain's lineage. The only thing that separates the two lineages was that one knew how to properly deal with his sin (Abel, Genesis 4:4) and the other let sin rule them (Cain, Genesis 4:6-7).

Furthermore, the New Testament contains Scriptures that many believe are related to the events of Genesis 6. In 2 Peter, Peter describes the angels who sinned as being locked up in gloomy darkness in hell until the Day of Judgment.

> "For if God did not spare angels when they sinned, but cast them into hell and committed them to chains of gloomy darkness to be kept until the judgment; if he did not spare the ancient world, but preserved Noah, a herald of righteousness, with seven others, when he brought a flood upon the world of the ungodly" (2 Peter 2:4-5).

Jude writes something similar to what Peter wrote. He states that

> "...the angels who did not stay within their own position of authority, but left their proper dwelling, he has kept in eternal chains under gloomy darkness until the judgment of the great day— just as Sodom and Gomorrah and the surrounding cities, which likewise indulged in sexual immorality and pursued unnatural desire, serve as an example by undergoing a punishment of eternal fire" (Jude 1:6-7).

Some scholars believe that these angels Peter and Jude are addressing are not the same ones that left with Satan (Ephesians 6:12; Revelation 12:3-4). These angels are locked up while Satan's angels are known as the evil spiritual beings or demonic spirits that are still actively tempting mankind today. In each passage, the authors give enough description to provide clarity regarding the type of spirits they're referring to.

In Peter's letter, the verse after he mentions the angels is about Noah and the flood. This means there is a progression to what he is writing. In other words, Peter addresses the angels that fell first because it precedes the flood. On the other hand, Jude follows up his description of the demonic spirits with a verse about the sexual sin that Sodom and Gomorrah committed and how they were judged for it.

When Jude addresses Sodom and Gomorrah, he uses the word "likewise", thereby connecting the sins the angels committed with that of Sodom and Gomorrah. This sin was sexual immorality. Within this understanding, we have probable reason to believe that Jude is referencing the events of Genesis 6 when he's talking about the angels being locked up in gloomy darkness.

Another key point in this argument is the fact that this sinful sexual act gave birth to giants. Solomon was righteous, so why did his betrothal to ungodly women not give birth to giants (1 Kings 3)? There more examples where a righteous man had sex with an unrighteous woman yet they did not produce giants.

Lastly, the term *sons of God,* in other places in the Old Testament, is only used in reference to angelic beings (Job 1:6; 2:1; 38:7). This term is found most in the book of Job. One particular place where this term is used is in Job 38.

After Job tries to defend his righteousness against his accusatory friends, God finally interjects and begins to admonish Job. It is during this discourse that God mentions the sons of God.

> "Where were you when I laid the foundation of the earth? Tell me, if you have understanding. Who determined its measurements—surely you know! Or who stretched the line upon it? On what were its bases sunk, or who laid its cornerstone, when the morning stars sang together and all the sons of God shouted for joy?" (Job 38:4-7).

Approximately one-third of the Hebrew Bible is poetry, and the book of Job is part of Hebrew poetic literature. Unlike poems in English that rhyme, Hebrew poems use ideas that rhyme. This type of poetry is known as synonymous parallelism[34].

In this passage, God is speaking to Job and He mentions the *morning stars* and *the sons of God.* This is a prime example of synonymous parallelism because it's referring to the same idea. The *morning stars* are angels and the *sons of God* are also angels. Furthermore, no human being was there when the earth was being founded, so contextually speaking, this verse can only be referring to angelic beings.

With this in mind, we can conclude that both Cain's and Seth's lineages were not perfect, and the only difference between the two was that one knew what to do with their sins while the other could care less. When we examine the way the New Testament writers referenced Genesis 6, we see that the sons of God and daughters of men gave birth to giants. Finally, the term *sons of God* throughout the Old Testament only was used for angels, and it's the same for Genesis 6. With this understanding, we can better understand the meaning of the whole text.

> "When man began to multiply on the face of the land and daughters were born to them, the sons of God saw that the daughters of man were

> attractive. And they took as their wives any they chose. Then the Lord said, "My Spirit shall not abide in man forever, for he is flesh: his days shall be 120 years." The Nephilim were on the earth in those days, and also afterward, when the sons of God came in to the daughters of man and they bore children to them. These were the mighty men who were of old, the men of renown. The Lord saw that the wickedness of man was great in the earth, and that every intention of the thoughts of his heart was only evil continually. And the Lord regretted that he had made man on the earth, and it grieved him to his heart. So the Lord said, "I will blot out man whom I have created from the face of the land, man and animals and creeping things and birds of the heavens, for I am sorry that I have made them" (Genesis 6:1-7).

Sons of God, or *benē hā'ĕlōhīm* (בְנֵי־הָאֱלֹהִים) in Hebrew[35], had sex with the daughters of men and gave birth to beings that were half-angel and half-men. These beings were known as the Nephilim (Genesis 6:1-4). Now the Bible states that these beings were there before the flood and after the flood. How they made it through the flood is a bit of a mystery.

It's possible that their genetics were passed down through one of Noah's daughter-in-laws, or that the flood didn't destroy all of them. Whatever the case may be, they survived and also had offspring.

Genesis 14 lists off most of the tribes that had giants in them after the flood.

> "In the fourteenth year Kedorlaomer and the kings who were with him came and defeated the Rephaim in Ashteroth-Karnaim, and the Zuzim in Ham, and the Emim in Shaveh-Kiriathaim, And the Horites in their

> hill country of Seir, as far as El-Paran, which is at the wilderness. Then they turned back and came to En-Mishpat (that is, Kadesh). And they defeated the whole territory of the Amalekites, and also the Amorites who were living in Hazazon-Tamar" (Genesis 14:5-7 LEB).

The first giants mentioned are the Rephaim (רְפָאִים) also known as "the terrible ones". Rephaim is the most common word used for giants, and in Deuteronomy 3, we get a great description of one of the Rephaim.

> "(For only Og, king of Bashan, was left from the remnant of the Rephaim. Indeed, his bedstead—it was a bedstead of iron. It is in Rabbah of the Ammonites. Nine cubits is its length, and four cubits is its width according to the cubit of a man.)…And the remainder of Gilead and all of Bashan, the kingdom of Og, I gave to the half-tribe of Manasseh, the whole region of Argo. All of that area of Bashan was called the land of the Rephaim" (Deuteronomy 3:11, 13 LEB).

King Og, who was a Rephaim, had a bed or coffin that was 13.5 feet long and 6 feet wide. The whole area where he lived was called "the land of the Rephaim" (v.13). Moses and the children of Israel slayed him and his children (Deuteronomy 1:4).

The Rephaim were also referred to as the Zamzummim or Zuzim (rooted in the Hebrew word *Zimzum* which meant "buzz, hum or muttering" and refers to the sound that ghost would make) (Isaiah 8:19). Another name for them was the Emim. The Hebrew root word for this name is *Eima* (אימה) which means "terror or fear". In modern Hebrew, "Seret Eima" {סרט אימה} means "horror film" and can teach us about how the ancient Moabites perceived the Rephaim[36].

Moses wrote about the Zamzummim when he gave instructions to the Israelites about the land of Ammon. In Deuteronomy 2, he told them that it was also considered the land of Rephaim because

> "Rephaim lived in it previously, and the Ammonites called them Zamzummim, a people great and numerous and as tall as the Anakites; Yahweh destroyed them from before them, and they dispossessed them and settled in place of them," (Deuteronomy 2:20-21 LEB).

Moses described the Zuzim as being as tall as the Anakites. Who were the Anakites? According to Scripture, the children of Israel believed them to be the descendants of the Nephilim. The spies who were sent to scope out the promised land came back and reported that they had seen giants.

> "And they presented the report of the land that they explored to the Israelites, saying, "The land that we went through to explore is a land that eats its inhabitants, and all the people whom we saw in its midst are men of great size. There we saw the Nephilim (the descendants of Anak came from the Nephilim), and we were like grasshoppers in our own sight, and so we were in their eyes" (Numbers 13:32-33 LEB).

This passage makes it very clear that the children Israel believed that "the descendants of Anak came from the Nephilim" (v. 33). The Zuzim who were still the Rephaim, therefore, were giants of the same stature, meaning they had the same genetics as well. In other words, we can conclude based on the evidence that the Rephaim were descendants of the Nephilim also.

Other giants that were descendants of the Nephilim were Goliath and his brothers. In the book of Joshua, the Israelites entered the promised land, and Joshua defeated the Anakim. While he devoted all of their belongings to destruction, he did not destroy all of the Anakites. Scripture states that none of the Anakites were left in the land of the Israelites, but that "some remained only in Gaza, Gath, and Ashdod" (Joshua 11:22 LEB)

The lands of Gaza, Gath, and Ashdod, in accordance with Joshua 11:22, had giants living in them. Goliath came from Gath[37]. This is clear evidence that Goliath had family ties to the Anakites, thus making him a descendant of the Nephilim.

The root meaning of the word *Rephaim* is two-fold-the Hebrew word *Rapha* which means "recovery, medicine, or cure", and the Hebrew word *Rapa*, which means "to sink down"[38]. The word for *doctor* in Hebrew is the word *Rophe* (רופא). Rophe is connected with an ancient belief that the 'Rephaim' had unique abilities to heal themselves[39].

In Israel, there is even a valley named Emeq Rephaim (עמק רפאים), or "the valley of the Rephaim". Likewise, Rephaim is the word used for "ghost" in Hebrew. In Israel, people use the phrase, "*We don't see ghosts today on Emek (Rephaim) Street"*[40] (לא רואים שדים היום ברחוב עמק רפאים). Likewise, sometimes the Bible replaces words like death, Sheol, Hades, and idol with Rephaim (Job 26:5 Psalms 88:10; Proverbs 2:18; Proverbs 9:18; Proverbs 21:16; Isaiah 14:9; Isaiah 26:14,19).

How does all this information on giants connect with demons? The connection lies with the spirits of the Nephilim and their closest descendants.

When Jude writes about the angels being locked up in judgment, he is referencing 1 Enoch.

Although the book of Enoch is no longer considered a canonical book, it was read during the time of Jesus and the apostles often quoted from it. While I'm not seeking to canonize it, I am keeping in step with the different quotations the apostles referenced, most of which had to do with angels having relationships with daughters of men.

Some commentators believe that Paul was referencing both Genesis 6 *and* the book of Enoch when he stated that a wife "ought to have a symbol of authority on her head, because of the angels" (1 Corinthians 11:10)[41]. This verse, along with 2 Peter 2:4 and Jude 1:5, supports the content of Genesis 6 and what Enoch covers on this subject. Understandably, then, we must read what Enoch says about this subject to better understand the context of this idea.

> And it came to pass when the children of men had multiplied that in those days were born to them beautiful and fair daughters. And the angels, the sons of heaven, saw and lusted after them, and said to one another: 'Come, let us choose us wives from among the children of men…And all of them together went and took wives for themselves, each choosing one for himself, and they began to go in to them and to defile themselves with sex with them, and the angels taught them charms and spells, and the cutting of roots, and made them acquainted with plants. And the women became pregnant, and they bare large giants, whose height was three thousand cubits (ells)…And then Michael, Uriel, Raphael, and Gabriel looked down from heaven and saw much blood being shed on the earth, and all lawlessness being done on the earth…And the women have borne giants, and the whole earth has

thereby been filled with blood and unrighteousness…The whole earth has been corrupted through the works that were taught by Azazel: to him ascribe ALL SIN.' To Gabriel said the Lord: 'Proceed against the bastards and the reprobates, and against the children of fornication and destroy the children of fornication and the children of the Watchers. Cause them to go against one another that they may destroy each other in battle: Shorten their days…Approach and hear my voice. Go and say to the Watchers of heaven, for whom you have come to intercede: "You should intercede for men, and not men for you." Why and for what cause have you left the high, holy, and eternal heaven, and had sex with women, and defiled yourselves with the daughters of men and taken to yourselves wives, and done like the children of earth, and begotten giants (as your) sons? Though you were holy, spiritual, living the eternal life, you have defiled yourselves with the blood of women, and have begotten children with the blood of flesh, and, as the children of men, you have lusted after flesh and blood like those who die and are killed…And now, the giants, who are produced from the spirits and flesh, shall be called evil spirits on the earth, and shall live on the earth. Evil spirits have come out from their bodies because they are born from men and from the holy Watchers; their beginning is of primal origin; they shall be evil spirits on earth, and evil spirits shall they be called spirits of the evil ones. [As for the spirits of heaven, in heaven shall be their dwelling, but as for the spirits of the earth which were born on the earth, on the earth shall be their dwelling.] And the spirits of the giants afflict, oppress, destroy, attack, war, destroy, and cause trouble on the earth.

(1 Enoch 6:1-2; 7:1; 9:1, 9-10; 10:9; 15:8-10)[42]

The watchers that Enoch mentions here are the "sons of God" found in Genesis 6. In addition, the writer of Enoch discusses that after the ungodly union between the daughters of men and these angels took place, their offspring were the Nephilim (giants) and in them they had nine evil spirits, which I believe are what we now refer to as demons (for more on this, please read Michael Heiser's book *Demons: What the Bible Really Says about the Powers of Darkness).*

These spirits were cursed to roam on the earth and to be inside the earth. According to the book of Enoch they "afflict, oppress, attack, war, destroy, and cause trouble on the earth" (1 Enoch 15:10).

Proverbs 9:18 says, "But he knoweth not that the dead are there; and that her guests are in the depths of hell" (וְלֹא־יָדַע כִּי־רְפָאִים שָׁם בְּעִמְקֵי שְׁאוֹל קְרֻאֶיהָ׃ פ). Here, Solomon is speaking about those who are lured by a temptress woman, and if you read this verse in Hebrew, you would see that it's connected to the evil spirits of the offspring of the Watchers. The word for *dead* here in Hebrew is Rephaim (רְפָאִים), and I do believe it's referring to evil spirits.

As one commentary explains it, "There are none "there," in her house, who can be said to be living; they are Rephaim, shadowy ghosts of living men, or else demons of the nether world."[43]. Solomon is not just saying the dead rotten corpse are her guests, but rather demons. It is a sharper warning; literally, those who are lured and have sex outside of marriage and watch pornography are doing it with demonic spirits.

Prayer

1 Samuel 17:46-47 states,

"This day the Lord will deliver you into my hand, and I will strike you down and cut off your head. And I will give the dead bodies of the host of the Philistines this day to the birds of the air and to the wild beasts of the earth, that all the earth may know that there is a God in Israel, and that all this assembly may know that the Lord saves not with sword and spear. For the battle is the Lord's, and he will give you into our hand".

Lord Jesus, the demons have set their eyes on me to harm me. They are the giants of old who sought to destroy Your world. As David defeated Goliath of Gath, I ask for your power to defeat these giants again! The Rephaim are tormenting me at night time, causing me to have nightmares night terrors. Lord Jesus, rid me of them! Deliver me from them! Let their oppression lift off of me! Free me from them! As David cut the head off Goliath, may all the Rephaim that have arisen against me meet the same fate as Goliath did in the name of Jesus! Amen!

Chapter 10 Questions

1. What is a Nephilim?

2. Why does the author believe the Nephilim were not just human beings?

3. What does the word Rephaim mean? How are the Rephaim connected to demons?

Chapter 11

MY JOURNEY TO FREEDOM

~~~

The first time it happened it was not planned. I walked into the room and started playing games. Then it just happened before I knew it.

I left that house feeling terrible. I couldn't believe what I'd done. *How did I get here?* One second I was looking at porn; the next second I was doing the unthinkable.

My dreams began to be unpleasant as well. They were very sexual. Sometimes I would be having sex with someone of the same gender and would wake up and my sheets would be wet.

My mind was perverted. Inconceivable thoughts would flood my mind every day. I watched so much porn that I could just play it in my mind and experience an orgasm from my thoughts.

I wanted to stop, but I felt powerless to do so. Not too long after vowing I would not go over to a certain person's house, I found myself back there. This
~~~

person was older than me by about three years. I really tried to fight these feelings I had inside, but I couldn't overcome them.

I lived a double life. At school I was Mr. Popular; at home I was depressed. I had no real desire to live at all. I thought God had wasted His breath on me.

Every single time I engaged in sexual activities, I wanted to quit. I would tell myself that this was the last time, but it wouldn't be the last. I would inevitably find myself back at this person's house, doing the same thing. I would feel gross afterward, but I knew I would be back.

I started to fight within myself. *Maybe this is my future. Maybe this is the way I was born.* The devil's scheme was working; he had created a path for me to walk on, a path towards death.

I remember my mom would always take us to prayer meetings. I was curious about God but scared to approach Him because of the darkness I had inside. I would feel so ashamed when I went. I would cry out to the God of my mom for mercy in hopes he would forgive me. Yet the more I watched porn, the more sexually hungry I became. I would get to the point where what I saw on the screen just wasn't enough and when I wanted more, I would go over to the house that I both hated and lusted for so much.

After I'd had my fix, I would head home crying and full of shame. My mom talked about the light, but all I felt was darkness. It was hard for me to sleep with the light off because I was afraid the evil spirits would come.

When I turned off the light to go to sleep, sometimes I could feel them. The darkness would move, overshadow me, and shadows from below would come on me with unfathomable weight and cause my body to freeze. It was not just a dream. The level of torment I experienced made me feel like I was in hell's prison cell.

Sometimes these entities would close up my airways and I wouldn't be able to breathe. I felt paralyzed. I would try to talk but my mouth wouldn't work. Sometimes, my eyes would be open and I would see things moving in my room. However, I couldn't speak or scream. I would remember my mom talking about her God and how she would call on Him when she was in trouble.

I would try to do the same. Since I couldn't speak it out loud I would say "Jesus" in my mind over and over and over until it finally came out my mouth, "*JESUS*!!!!". And immediately whatever was holding me down and causing me to be paralyzed would liberate me.

I started praying to my mom's God more often. I knew deep down inside that only He could stop me from going to this person's house. So for three years, almost every night, I would cry out to this God that I did not know and ask Him to deliver me.

I remember the last time I went to this guy's house. When I left, I felt strength inside of me to say to myself out loud, "I will never go back to this house again." I knew this wasn't something I had conjured up; I knew something was causing me to not go back and empowering me to say no!

My dreams began to change, and my confusion left. Jesus freed me completely from homosexuality. Years later, after I became a Christian, God also delivered me from pornography. While the deliverance from homosexuality came suddenly, the deliverance from pornography took years of battling before I truly walked in freedom.

Not everything we struggle with will be overcome instantly, which is why we should never stop fighting. My freedom from pornography started with going through a book one of my college professors gave me called *The Bondage Breaker* by Dr. Neil T. Anderson.

Reading this book was not easy. When I first tried to read it, I would immediately fall asleep. The devil clearly did not want me to walk in total freedom. But I kept pressing forward, even though it was hard, and I kept reading until I finished the book. I realized that many of the accusatory thoughts that were in my mind were just the devil trying to oppress me.

I did not get completely free after reading this book, but through this book I realized that freedom was part of the believer's inheritance and truth is greater than lies!

> "So Jesus said to the Jews who had believed him, "If you abide in my word, you are truly my disciples, and you will know the truth, and the truth will set you free."" (John 8:31-32).

Many people quote the latter part of this verse and they miss the full meaning. Jesus was not just telling anyone that they would know the truth and the truth would set them free. The Bible says He was speaking to Jews who believed, which means you have to believe in Jesus.

Secondly, Jesus said "if you abide in My Word." Abiding in something means you live in it, you love it. This verse could be likened to Psalms 1:2 that states, “but his delight is in the law of the Lord, and on his law he meditates day and night” (Psalm 1:2).

Abiding in His word means you think about it continuously every day. Jesus said someone is truly His disciple when they are abiding in His word. This means there has to be more than just head knowledge-you must actually follow Jesus.

It’s only after these principles are established in our lives that we get to know the truth and it truly liberates us. It was only when I submitted to God’s will fully and chose to genuinely be His disciple, to pursue Jesus, and to apply the truths I learned through *The Bondage Breaker* to my life, that I began to experience true freedom.

After I finished *The Bondage Breaker,* the Holy Spirit spoke to me about the importance of meditating on the Scriptures. He took me to Psalm 119:9-11:

> “How can a young man keep his way pure? By guarding it according to your word. With my whole heart I seek you; let me not wander from your commandments! I have stored up your word in my heart, that I might not sin against you.”

After reading these verses, I set up an alarm clock for 4 am and reached out to my friends for prayer and accountability. The Holy Spirit told me to commit to not quit and to refuse to walk in guilt.

Also, my wife Katie, whom I was courting at the time, told me to get rid of my computer. I threw it in the trash. Sometimes when we pray, we think our prayers will sweep in and save us when part of our solution is also practical. If you're struggling with pornography and you still have a computer or electronic device you use without accountability, then you are not serious about being free.

With all this in mind I began my journey toward freedom. I felt that I needed to meditate on all of the book of Jude. Meditation, the Holy Spirit showed me, was different then simple memorization.

We are meant to imitate what we meditate on instead of being mesmerized by what we memorize. This means that when we're meditating on Scripture, we are actively seeking to live out what we are memorizing, not just trying to remember it. Day by day, verse by verse, I'd chew on the Word of God.

The more I pushed towards my freedom, the more the devil ramped up his attacks. Whenever I was experiencing a long period of freedom, sexual demons would show up in my dreams and violate me. I'd wake up with my sheets wet as if someone had physically had sex with me.

But I was determined to be free, so I kept going. I continuously stored up the Word of God in my heart and believed it to be my daily food. Yet six months later, I experienced disappointment. I fell into sexual sin again.

Discouraged, I brought my complaints to God. I heard God speak to my heart and say, "Gloire, you've been trying to do this on your own strength. How has it been going?"

He reminded me of Jude 1:24 that says that it's Him "who is able to keep [us] from stumbling and to present [us] blameless before the presence of his glory with great joy,". God highlighted to me the fact that *He* was the one who was able to keep me from stumbling and present me blameless before the presence of His glory, and that He takes great joy in doing it!

This revelation came through me abiding in His Word. The Word of God is the sharpest double-edged sword. It pierces you (Hebrews 4:12) and it cuts the enemy (Revelation 1:16). In Ephesians 6, when it talks about the "sword of the spirit, which is the word of God," the Greek word for *word* is *rhema* which means "the spoken word".

As I was declaring the Word of God out loud during my meditation time, it went from the logos word (the written word) to the activated Word. Picture a sword in its sheath-this represents the written word. When the sword is drawn and is being used, it becomes the rhema spoken Word.

Although I would go on to fall several more times, after Jesus assured me that He is the one who truly frees us, I knew He had delivered me from pornography. It's been many years now since I've struggled with pornography. I am completely free, and you can be too!

Those sexual spirits never gave up on enticing me. Every now and then they'd show up in my dreams disguised as a gorgeous woman. By the grace of God, as I admitted my faults to God and my accountability partners, submitted my whole heart to God, and resisted the devil through using the sword of the spirit (the Word of God). I rebuked these entities in Jesus' name, and they fled!

These sexual demons cannot hide anymore. I've now realized that God has graciously exposed their operations through their attacks on my life. I now know who they are.

Nothing sexual we see today is new. The false gods of old were all sexually deviant. Some of them had sex with both male and female partners. Isn't it kind of odd that many people who are experiencing this "sexual revolution" connect most with Greek gods?

Hermaphrodites was the offspring of Hermes and Aphrodite. Tradition tells us that Hermaphrodites inherited both of his parents' beauty. He grew up with nymphs who were of a large class of lesser female divinities, sometimes associated with things that grew (like trees or water)[44].

While he was with the nymphs, a nymph of the well loved him earnestly and tried to win him over but could not. One day while Hermaphrodites was bathing in the well, this nymph prayed to the gods to be merged with Hermaphrodites and the gods granted his prayer.

Afterwards, "the bodies of the youth and the nymph became united in such a manner that the two together could not be called either a man or a woman, but were both. Hermaphroditus, on becoming aware of the change, prayed that in future everyone who bathed in the well should be metamorphosed into an hermaphrodite."[45]

This is no longer just a myth we read about but has become a reflection of our society. Demons of old are still operating today, as Solomon said, "What has been is what will be, and what has been done is what will be done, and there is nothing new under the sun" (Ecclesiastes 1:9).

The gods and goddesses of old are the demons of today, appearing as various kinds of creatures of the night and seducing men, women, and children alike. The Bible mentioned many of these creatures that different cultures at times called “gods”.

For years, they hid themselves in movies and children’s books, making us laugh and cry all the while beguiling us. But no longer will we be their victims- it's time to expose these creatures of the night and expel them!

Prayer

"O Lord, you have searched me and known me! You know when I sit down and when I rise up; You discern my thoughts from afar. You search out my path and my lying down and are acquainted with all my ways. Even before a word is on my tongue, behold, O Lord, You know it altogether. You hem me in, behind and before, and lay Your hand upon me. Such knowledge is too wonderful for me; it is high; I cannot attain it. Where shall I go from Your Spirit? Or where shall I flee from Your presence? If I ascend to heaven, You are there! If I make my bed in Sheol, You are there! If I take the wings of the morning and dwell in the uttermost parts of the sea, even there Your hand shall lead me, and Your right hand shall hold me. If I say, "Surely the darkness shall cover me, and the light about me be night," even the darkness is not dark to you; the night is bright as the day, for darkness is as light with You. For You formed my inward parts; You knitted me together in my mother's womb. I praise You, for I am fearfully and wonderfully made. Wonderful are Your works; my soul knows it very well. My frame was not hidden from You, when I was being made in secret, intricately woven in the depths of the earth. Your eyes saw my unformed substance; in Your book were written, every one of them, the days that were formed for me, when as yet there was none of them. How precious to me are Your thoughts, O God! How vast is the sum of them! If I would count them, they are more than the sand. I awake, and I am still with you" (Psalm 139:1-18).

Lord, you made me, You formed me, You know me. The enemy has tried to deceive and cause me to believe that the identity that You created me with is the wrong one. He has brought confusion into my mind. The world around me is also pushing Satan's agenda on me, telling me that I can identify as whatever I want to identify as. But I say no to the lies of the evil one and all his henchmen!

I rebuke the scheme of the devil for my life! Lord, You know my identity; please reveal it to me! Please rid me of the spirit of homosexuality and gender confusion. Please cleanse my thoughts from pornography! Set me free from pornography addiction. Give me a desire for Your Word so I can read and meditate on it! I desperately need You, Jesus! I confess that I love the pleasures of this world more than I love You. Please help me to hate the things of this world and to love You! Free me from pornography and gender confusion! Free me Lord Jesus!

"You make known to me the path of life; in your presence there is fullness of joy; at your right hand are pleasures forevermore" (Psalm 16:11). Please make known my path Lord Jesus. Fill me with the joy from Your presence and give me your pleasure so I'll never desire worldly pleasures anymore! In Jesus' name I pray, amen!

Chapter 11 Questions

1. What are the two things the author struggled with?

2. How did the authors first struggle begin?

3. What were the steps the author used to be free from his second struggle?

Chapter 12

CREATURES OF THE NIGHT

~~~

To truly expose demonic entities, we must understand the truth about idols. All idols are connected to the demonic world (1 Corinthians 10:20). This means any god other than the biblical God is a demonic entity.

Oftentimes when I've taken people through deliverance, I've been amazed at how the demons that manifested were all connected somehow to foreign gods, especially the ones found in Greek mythology. After Alexander the Great's conquest, Greek culture spread everywhere. Legend tells us that "an Egyptian king, Ptolemy Philadelphus (reigned from 285-246 BCE), commissioned a translation of the Hebrew Bible for his library in Alexandria. Seventy-two translators from Jerusalem were subsequently sent to the Island of Pharos to translate the Torah into Greek.

The term Septuagint, which means "seventy," actually refers to the seventy-two translators—six from each tribe of Israel—involved in translating the Pentateuch from Hebrew to Greek in the third-century BCE. Seventy-two is rounded down to seventy, hence the Roman numeral LXX[46].
~~~

Legends aside, the Septuagint is a real biblical manuscript, broken up into several different manuscripts. It is one of the oldest copies of the biblical texts we have, dating back to before the time Jesus was here on earth. It's not a perfect copy of the biblical text, nor is there a perfect copy that exists today. Only the original sources were perfect. It is, however, the most quoted work by New Testament writers, which for me solidifies that its translation was divinely influenced by the Spirit of God.

As you read through the Septuagint, you can see that the scribes who translated the biblical text understood that much of Greek mythology coincided with the biblical view of demonology. When Paul went to Athens, he saw a statue-less inscription written to an unknown god, and he used it as a way to connect the people of that culture to the true God. Likewise, the scribes took what they had seen in Greek culture and helped their Jewish audience better understand the biblical text. They knew it had to be biblically accurate and culturally relevant.

One specific place the scribes did this was in Isaiah 13:21. In this verse the scribes translated "the daughters of ostriches" to mean *seirēnes*, or *sirens*. Why? I believe that since they were translating from an older text than we have, they understood that the context was more supernatural since the verse continues and says these creatures will be "dancing with daimonia (demons)". Many modern translations say "goats" with a clear understanding that the word *goat* is connected to a demon named "Satyrs."

Understandably, then, if the word *goat* symbolizes demonic forces, then the other creatures must follow suit if we are to stay in context. These are creatures of the night; not only natural, but shadows of evil spirits. This verse can also be connected to Isaiah 34:14, which in Hebrew calls the "screeching owls" Lilith (לִילִית).

As folklore has it, Lilith was the first wife of Adam, who ended up divorcing him, spouting off God's name, then sprouting wings and moving to the Red Sea. While at the Red Sea, she gave birth to many demon children who were killed by three angels. Enraged, she turned her eyes on every child 1-20 years old and to men.

She made it her mission to kill the children and seduce the men at night, terrorizing them with nightmares[47]. This, of course, is traditionally passed down and not Scripturally accurate. However, I believe Lilith is still a real demonic entity.

Lilith could be connected to what many call a *succubus*- a female demon who fornicates with men at night. The counterpart of *succubus* is an *incubus,* which is a male sexual demon who commits sexual acts with women[48]. An example of this would be the satyrs, who we will look at later in this chapter.

The book of Tobit, which is another non-canonical book of the Bible written around the third or second century B.C, mentions the existence of an incubus demon known as Asmodeus. The book of Tobit shares a story about the demon Asmodeus, who was a lustful, sexually immoral, demonic being who in pursuit of a woman by the name of Sarah, killed seven of her husbands (Tobit 3 GNTA).

Having experienced these sexual attacks firsthand, I know that although the stories of Lilith, the satyrs, the sirens, and Asmodeus may be embellished, they are rooted in spiritual reality. Demons are constantly doing their wicked acts among us. We must not be ignorant of their devices or else we will be outwitted by them (2 Corinthians 2:11).

Let us then take a deeper look at what sirens are and how they operate. In Greek mythology, sirens are not the same as the ones most commonly known by many cultures as mermaids or mermen. They were actually a hybrid being-half-woman and half-bird.

The bottom half of a siren was the lower half of a bird, and the top half was a woman with the wings of a bird. They would lure men in with their enchanted songs and kill them.

The Septuagint, which was the Bible that Jesus and the disciples used and quoted from, it clearly depicts these entities as demonic creatures. The following is the passage in both English and Greek that speaks about the sirens:

> And shall rest there wild beasts, and they shall fill up the houses with a sound; and shall rest there sirens and demons will dance there (Isaiah 13:21 Interlinear Study Bible)

> καὶ ἀναπαύσονται (anapausontai) ἐκεῖ (ekei) θηρία (thēria) καὶ ἐμπλησθήσονται (emplēsthēsontai) αἱ (hai) οἰκίαι (oikiai) ἤχου (ēchou) καὶ ἀναπαύσονταιθ (anapausontai) ἐκεῖ (ekei) σειρῆνες (seirēnes) καὶ δαιμόνια (daimonia) ἐκεῖ (ekei) ὀρχήσονται, orchēsontai[49].

In this chapter, Isaiah is prophesying about the destruction of Babylon many years before it arose to its dominant stature. It is during this prophetic announcement that he states (in the Septuagint) that sirens and demons (satyrs) will dwell, or rest, in Babylon at her destruction.

Most commentaries do not translate this verse like the Septuagint does. The Enduring Word Commentary summarizes the thoughts of many of the commentators on this verse and gives their overall understanding of it.

> "Owls...ostriches...wild goats...hyenas: The animals mentioned here are impossible to identify precisely. The picture is of the darkness and confusion surrounding the fall of Babylon. The 'wild goats' (v. 21) are sometimes associated with demons in goat form that are called 'satyrs' (Leviticus 17:7; 2 Chronicles 11:15)."[50]

I think the best way to concretely interpret this verse is to merge the two together. What the Enduring Word Commentary states is impossible to identify precisely; I believe the Septuagint identified it as "seirēnes." Likewise, what the Septuagint calls "demons" is further expounded on as 'satyrs'- demons whose bottom half looks like a goat with an erected penis and whose top half is a man with goat's horns and horse-like ears[51].

Satyrs were known as the fertility gods of the woodlands, which means they actually caused barrenness. It's important to keep in mind that whenever a god other than the God of the Bible is known for doing something positive, the opposite is actually true. Satyrs had an unquenchable sexual appetite. These creatures would at times rape the nymphs and sometimes women, as well as have sex with animals[52].

They were associated with the Greek god Dionysus, the god of wine and debauchery, and Pan, the god who was so frightful that "panic attacks" are named after him. I'll even go further and say that panic attacks are also maintained and sometimes caused by this demon[53].

Another thing Pan was associated with was child molestation. At Banias (originally spelled *Panias* after the god Pan) in Caesarea Philippi, Jesus asked the disciples who the people were saying He was. After the disciples gave different answers, Simon Peter said, "…You are the Christ, the Son of the living God" (Matthew 16:16).

Jesus applauds him and then states, "And I tell you, you are Peter, and on this rock I will build my church, and the gates of hell shall not prevail against it" (Matthew 16:18). The "gates of hell" Jesus was speaking about, I believe, is all of Satan's kingdom. Jesus makes this statement purposefully, as geographically-speaking, they were located right next to a cavern at the base of Mount Hermon, which was the mountain that the rebellious angels from Genesis 6 descended upon (1Enoch 6:6). Thus, it is a spiritual gate; an access point for demonic activity. There was an altar inside this cavern they used to sacrifice babies to the demonic god Pan, making it portal to the netherworld[54].

Jesus came to this specific spot a place filled with darkness, a place that some say was the place where the malevolent angels fell in their rebellion against God. This was also a place where Pan, one the worst of the gods, was worshipped. It is here that Jesus established His church and proclaimed the gospel of the Kingdom of God.

This is His weapon here on earth that the gates of hell will not prevail against! Declaring war on the would-be gods and giving the church authority to loose and bind- terms that are central to the gospel message. "I will give you the keys of the kingdom of heaven, and whatever you bind on earth shall be bound in heaven, and whatever you loose on earth shall be loosed in heaven" (Matthew 16:19).

This power meant that the church, through the gospel of Jesus Christ, can give allowance to things here on earth and it shall be done in Heaven. The church shall also disallow things and it shall be disallowed in Heaven. But what is the meaning of this?

The binding and loosing that the church does disarms the principalities and authorities. How? It gives access to the gospel to those who are near and those who are far off (Ephesians 2:17). In Acts 2:14-40, Peter uses the key Jesus gave the church to open the door to the kingdom by proclaiming the gospel to all the Jews who would hear.

Then again in Acts 10, Peter uses the key Jesus gave the church to open the door to the Kingdom for the Gentiles. Through these two acts Peter did, the term binding meaning (not allowing access to), or loosing (allowing access to), was being accomplished. By proclaiming the gospel, Peter granted Kingdom access to those who did not have access before.

This power of binding and loosing allows the church to break the yoke of sin by pointing sinners to the One who canceled all of the record of sin and nailed it to the cross.

> "And you, who were dead in your trespasses and the uncircumcision of your flesh, God made alive together with him, having forgiven us all our trespasses, by canceling the record of debt that stood against us with its legal demands. This he set aside, nailing it to the cross. He disarmed the rulers and authorities and put them to open shame, by triumphing over them in him" (Colossians 2:13-15).

Jesus was emboldening the church and giving them His authority to no longer be bound by the legality of the law and no longer live by regulations such as "do not eat, touch". He was giving them the freedom and authority to live by the liberty of the Spirit of God (Colossians 2). This is a highly spiritual act!

While the law is good, sin gets empowered by the law because we can never accomplish the whole law. Thus, it produces death in us instead of life because through the law, we were condemned.

> "O death, where is your victory? O death, where is your sting?" The sting of death is sin, and the power of sin is the law. But thanks be to God, who gives us the victory through our Lord Jesus Christ" (1 Corinthians 15:55-57).

The principalities and authorities want to use legalism to keep believers stuck under the law, thus disarming the believer of his authority. It all has to do with the spiritual legal system. Binding and losing is a legal terminology.

In Jesus' culture, the Pharisees would use "binding and loosing" to establish new rules or excuse people from following others (Mark 7:11). The Pharisees and the spiritual leaders, however, did not have God's approval to bind and loose, but the church of today does.

Demonic forces know that if they are to keep us bound, we must not know our rights and must be kept isolated. But a powerful weapon against sexual sin and other sin is the deliverance that comes from the church collectively. I would argue that a believer who stays outside the church body and acts as a lone ranger will miss out on the fullness of deliverance.

It's hard to walk in the light when there is no one to hold you accountable. This power of binding and loosing was given to the whole church, not just certain individuals. Without confession, a person can never be free.

> "Therefore, confess your sins to one another and pray for one another, that you may be healed. The prayer of a righteous person has great power as it is working" (James 5:16).

It's important to announce the truth and renounce lies with trusted brothers and sisters who will pray for you so you can experience deliverance. Proverbs 28:13 states that a person who conceals his transgressions "will not prosper, but he who confesses and forsakes them will obtain mercy" (Proverbs 28:13). The enemy has power over you when you conceal acts of darkness.

Sexual sin always wants to stay hidden. It's cloaked in shame. But Jesus has given the church the authority necessary to allow the fullness of the grace and mercy of God to penetrate this darkness. It's important to expose lust and sexual thoughts to the body of believers and God will immediately or eventually give you full victory!

In conclusion, sirens, satyrs, Lilith, Pan, and Asmodeus, to list a few, are some of the demons behind a lot of the sexual perversion we see today. Sirens, satyrs, and many other demonic entities were going to dwell in Babylon when it was destroyed because it became a desolate and unclean place, which is the right environment for demonic spirits to dwell. They had the right, in other words, to be there.

When we see depravity in a place, we should seek to discern what gives demonic spirits the rights or access to a certain place or individual. In the following chapter, we are going to discuss other entities called marine spirits that are the cause of many evil circumstances in people's lives. It's time to expose them.

Prayer

I'm under attack, O God, I'm under attack! My mind is tormented by sexual thoughts. I am addicted to having sex. As David went after Bethsheba, I have gone after my sin. Please liberate me! I remember You speaking through Nathan the prophet:

> *"And I gave you your master's house and your master's wives into your arms and gave you the house of Israel and of Judah. And if this were too little, I would add to you as much more" (2 Samuel 12:8).*

And if it had been too little, You told him that You would have added more for him. Lord, I feel discontent with what I have. Lust makes me seek for more, but I want to trust You! I want to believe what You said to David! That You're a God who knows what I need, and if I need more, You will meet those needs! Teach me how to be content. Your Word says that "godliness with contentment is great gain, for we brought nothing into the world, and we cannot take anything out of the world. But if we have food and clothing, with these we will be content" (1 Timothy 6:6-8). May I be like Job, who said, "I have made a covenant with my eyes; how then could I gaze at a virgin?" (Job 31:1). Please deliver me from the incubus and succubus who are having sex with me at night, tormenting me in my dreams, and enticing my thoughts. In the mighty name of Jesus!! AMEN!

Chapter 12 Questions

1. What's a siren?

2. What is an incubus and succubus?

3. What do goats commonly represent in the Bible?

4. If a person does not get fully involved in a church body, they cannot ____.

5. What does binding and loosing mean?

Chapter 13

DR. MEL'S TESTIMONY

~~~~

My name is Dr. Mel, and I am a licensed physician, military veteran, mother, and most importantly, a daughter of the Most High God. This is my story of bondage, distortion of truth, destruction, and redemption and restoration.

Most of my life was spent in bondage to types of demons known as marine spirits. Some better know them as mermaids, mermen, or sirens. These spirits sound and appear beautiful and enticing but are really there to lure you to your death. The problem with these spirits is that you won't understand their purpose until you are so ensnared you cannot get yourself out.

My story begins when I was a child at about the age of five or six. My mother would babysit some children from the neighborhood, including two boys from across the street. The eldest of these boys was 13 years old and enjoyed being mean to me. He would pinch me and pull my hair until I cried and complained to my parents.
~~~~

My parents would always urge me to get along with him by saying, "he is only doing these things because you get upset," and "if you stop reacting, he will stop picking on you." Of course, none of these statements were true and I continually tried to not react to this boy. There were only so many pinches and hair pulls I could stand without crying.

One day after getting in trouble for "not getting along," these marine spirits used the opportunity to entice me. This boy approached me while I was in my bedroom and promised to be nice to me if I would do some things for him. He wanted it to be "our secret." For the first time since knowing this boy, he was not trying to make me cry. Though my spirit inside of me was screaming for me to run, I stayed to listen to his proposal because it seemed like we were "getting along."

This relationship developed into various forms of sexual abuse that continued for months. In the end, I was left with an open door for these spirits to manifest and wreak havoc on my life. The bondage started with masturbation, which was daily, even as a child, and progressed to morbid sexual fantasies. I fantasized about being sex trafficked before I knew such a thing existed. Images that flooded through my mind grew in grotesqueness as I aged and were full of things I had never even seen or heard of. Not only were the images there, but the door opened in my life allowed many other sexually abusive situations to take place. This led me to avoid men altogether and to purposely act and dress in a way that would be unattractive to them. I did this until the age of 16.

When I began dating at the age of 18, I was powerless to resist any man's sexual advancement toward me, and I began having sex outside of marriage to my first husband. It was not long until I became pregnant, and my not-yet husband knew I was pregnant before I showed any symptoms. He recommended we get an abortion and, in my shame and embarrassment from being pregnant outside of marriage, I agreed to the procedure. Part of me died that day, and I unknowingly fed these marine spirits with the sacrifice of my firstborn.

Their hold on me grew stronger. Soon after, I got married, and these spirits worked to destroy my marriage while continuing to entrap me in more lust and sexual perversion. My lust and bondage caused me to become bitter and angry towards my first husband, and I despised him. When an opportunity came to cheat on him, I did, justifying my actions with my hatred towards him. I destroyed my marriage, and with it, my son's spirit.

By this point in my life, I had given up on God and on the idea that He cared for me. I would like to point out that all these events and bondage in my life occurred *after* I knew Jesus as my Savior, not before. I prayed, went to church every time the church was open, was active in youth, served on missions, went to youth conventions, was baptized in the Holy Spirit with the evidence of speaking in tongues, and professed to be a Christian. All the while, I was completely bound.

After living one year completely avoiding God, I realized that my life was empty without Him. I began praying again but was not willing (or able) to give up my sinful ways. I had convinced myself that living with my boyfriend was fine because I had already been divorced, and that masturbating to fantasies was fine as long as I did not imagine anyone specific in my fantasies. Just to be clear, these "fantasies" were not anything I would want or desire to have done to me. They were grotesquely perverse and sexually abusive to the point I would be disgusted with myself for having these "fantasies." Although I grew up in church, no one had taught me that these types of thoughts did not originate from me, but from evil spirits. This is why Paul taught us to take every thought captive to the obedience of Christ (2 Corinthian 10:5).

As I began to pursue God, He began to unweave and loosen what the enemy had bound in my life. I broke up with an abusive boyfriend. I was still unable to resist my lust and was intimate with my current husband before we were married. While we were engaged, a man, whom I thought was a friend, drugged me and violently raped me to the point that I bled as if I were on my period. These spirits twisted my memory of this event to make it seem like I wanted or desired this. Because of the drugs that had been given to me, I did not even realize what had happened until the Lord revealed it to me.

After my husband and I married, lust ruled our relationship and drove nearly every sexual encounter that we had. I continued to pursue God, but every time I felt like I was getting closer to Him, these spirits would tighten their grip on me. At about this time in my life, I met Gloire, and he spoke of deliverance and freedom in Christ. God had been showing me in dreams that I would be doing deliverance and would be able to identify spirits, but I was so bound at the time that I couldn't discern my own thoughts. I asked to watch Gloire do a deliverance and participate, which he allowed me to do. Gloire correctly discerned my own bondage, which I had yet to realize.

He walked me through a book called *The Bondage Breaker*, which opened my eyes to how bound I had become. I began to try to resist these marine spirits by refusing to masturbate and trying to avoid thinking about these perverse sexual fantasies. I would succeed at times and fail at others, but every day I was tormented. When Gloire took me through deliverance, the spirits left, and the door of lust was closed in my life. Because I didn't address the actions and events that allowed the marine spirits access into my life, they were still operating, but were hidden. The need for masturbation and the daily sexually perverse fantasies were gone, but the spirits were still present and manifested themselves in my subconscious dreams, where I was weakest and struggled to resist them.

By the time I met Gloire, my husband and I had been trying to become pregnant for two years. We had experienced one miscarriage and an ectopic pregnancy. Over the course of the next six years, we would experience three more miscarriages. We were told by the OB/GYN who performed the ectopic pregnancy procedure that I would not be able to have children because of how twisted by Fallopian tubes were, which was a direct result of the violent rape that occurred.

After the last miscarriage, another minister we met named Jean made a point to take time to pray with me and take me through deliverance. Prior to this he had been talking to me about marine spirits. While he was speaking, I could feel them manifesting in my sexual organs. They would twist and turn and cause a burning sensation. When Jean would stop talking about the marine spirits, the sensation would cease. I believe God was using this to show me how and where these spirits were in operation in my life, which broke down my pride and allowed the opportunity for true deliverance. Together we prayed in two sessions. In the first session, God brought to light every sexual thing that had happened to me and every sexual thing I caused to happen. These marine spirits were bound, and many were cast out. I could feel the release from my womb.

The night after the first session, I conceived my son, Kavel. I was continuing to get attacked in my dreams, and the Lord used these dreams to reveal to me how much I hated men because of my past. With the help of the Holy Spirit, I forgave them and started the process of healing from these events in my life (which is still ongoing).

The second deliverance session occurred a couple months later, after I knew I was pregnant. During this deliverance, the plan of the enemy in my life was revealed as well as each step these marine spirits planned to use to block the birth of my child. First, they wanted to use marital discord between my husband and myself to prevent conception. If that failed, they had planned to take the life of the child with a miscarriage.

I had believed that because I aborted my first child, I was unworthy to have another baby. This was the door that allowed them access to my womb, which, when closed, prevented this plan in the future. Then, if the miscarriage failed, they would try to use the umbilical cord to take the life of the baby. Next, there was a plan to take my life with a car accident while I was pregnant. Finally, they planned to cause a complication during childbirth that would cause the death of myself and my baby.

All the plans of the marine spirits had been exposed and covered in prayer while these spirits were being cast out of me. Today, I am happy to announce that I have a healthy, happy, baby boy named Kavel (which means to "wait on God" or "God waits") who was conceived after the loss of five previous pregnancies. God is good and His mercies endure forever. I was redeemed and restored through His blood. I was bound and unable to bear children, now I am free and able to feel the joy of motherhood once again.

Chapter 14

THE MARINE SPIRITS

When you mention the term “marine spirits” in many Western churches, people will look at you like you’re out of your mind. Part of the reason is because these spirits aren’t known. For other cultures, marine spirits are a reality, but because they sometimes fail to explain biblically what they experience, it creates a lot of distrust with true Bible-believing churches. For many churches, if they don’t see these things in the Bible, they won’t trust it to be true.

Frankly, they are absolutely right. We must always have a solid Scriptural basis for the things we are claiming to be true. So what is a marine spirit? A marine spirit is a water demon. It’s a demonic spirit that inhabits the water, waiting for someone to open the door in their life so they can come in. Once they are in an individual, they hide and manipulate that person’s desires.

There are folktales that talk about there being marriages between mermaids, who would transform themselves into human beings, and men. What normally would happen in these folktales is the man would steal the marine spirit’s belt, cap, mirror, or comb. As long as the items were hidden, the mermaid would live with the man, but if she found the items, she would return immediately to the sea.

In different variations of the story, the marriage would last as long as the covenant that was made was kept, and it ended when the covenant was broken.

> "Their gifts brought misfortune, and, if offended, the beings caused floods or other disasters. To see one on a voyage was an omen of shipwreck. They sometimes lured mortals to death by drowning, as did the Lorelei of the Rhine, or enticed young people to live with them underwater, as did the mermaid whose image is carved on a bench in the church of Zennor, Cornwall, England."[55]

Where in the Bible do we find these beings? The first clear place is during the ten plagues. According to several commentaries, the plagues on Egypt were a judgment, not just on the nation of Egypt, but also on its gods.

Moreover, God Himself told Moses that He was judging the gods of Egypt. "I will strike all the firstborn in the land of Egypt, both man and beast; and on all the gods of Egypt I will execute judgments: I am the Lord" (Exodus 12:12).

The first plague saw the Nile turn into blood. If the plagues were also a judgment on the gods of Egypt, then what god was over the Nile? There were several: Hapi (Apis) male god of the Nile; Khnum, guardian of the Nile; Isis (Aset), goddess of the Nile; Osiris, and Heqet the frog-headed goddess. Apis was seen as an androgynous god (having both male and female characteristics) and was believed to aid in fertility.

Next there was Khnum, also an Egyptian god of fertility, followed by Isis, goddess of love, fertility, healing, magic, and the moon. Osiris was a god of fertility and the underworld, and Heqet (a marine spirit) was another goddess of fertility[56].

Do you see a similar trait to all these gods? Most gods or goddesses connected to the water were sought for help with fertility. Any god that is "over" something will often cause the opposite thing to happen. This is why an individual's ability to have a child is blocked by marine spirits.

Additionally, if one of these gods does fulfill something in your life, you will owe them. People end up paying for riches or other requests they make from these false gods by being cursed, experiencing sickness, or even death.

Another marine spirit in the Bible is Dagon, the god of the Philistines. Dagon's sculpture is the only one we read about in the Bible that was broken when the Ark of the LORD was placed in the same room (1 Samuel 5:3-4). What many westerners don't know about Dagon is that he is a merman-half man and half-fish.

Dagon was the god over crops and of course, fertility[57]. If idols represent their demonic counterparts, then the spirit that was connected to Dagon is a marine spirit, a water demon (Deuteronomy 32:16-17).

One of the main things that marine spirits use to destroy humans is sexual immorality. Delilah was a woman in the Bible whom I believe was demonized by a marine spirit.

The Bible says that Samson fell in love with her (Judges 16:1), but what's interesting is that you never read anywhere about Samson loving God. This could explain why eventually Sampson fell-he loved worldly pleasures more than God.

The name Delilah in Hebrew means "delicate and feeble". In other languages the name is associated with a worshiper of Ishtar, the pagan goddess. It's also a play on words because *lai'lah* (לַיְלָה), means "night". Samson's name, on the other hand, is derived from the word *shemesh,* which means "sun".

God had given Samson specific instructions about how he was to live. He had taken a Nazarite vow from birth and was not to drink anything that came from grapes (Judges 13). God knew that it was in the Valley of Sorek, a name related to grapes, that the sun (Samson) would encounter the night (Delilah) and the strong would be defeated by men's weakness: sexual immorality. Delilah was from the valley of Sorek (Judges 16)[58].

When the Philistines discovered that Samson and Delilah were together, they asked Delilah to seduce Samson and discover the source of his power. Each ruler of the Philistines agreed to pay her 1,100 pieces of silver (Judges 16:5).

After three attempts, Delilah eventually caused Samson to reveal the secret to his power, which was his hair (Judges 16:10-17). When she finished her mission, the Philistines paid her and praised their marine god Dagon (Judges 16:23-24). This is how marine spirits operate- they seduce people and cause them to lose sight of their purpose. Their main goals are to quench the anointing in people's lives, cause people to suffer, and separate people from God.

Samson was not the only person who was lured and conquered by marine spirits. Solomon was another man of God who was seduced and fell victim to them. The Bible says,

> "...when Solomon was old his wives turned away his heart after other gods, and his heart was not wholly true to the Lord his God, as was the heart of David his father. Then Solomon built a high place for Chemosh the abomination of Moab, and for Molech the abomination of the Ammonites, on the mountain east of Jerusalem. Therefore the Lord said to Solomon, "Since this has been your practice and you have not kept my covenant and my statutes that I have commanded you, I will surely tear the kingdom from you and will give it to your servant" (1 Kings 11:4-6, 7, 11).

Solomon saw the literal glory of God (2 Chronicles 5), God showed up to him in a dream (1 Kings 3:5) and Solomon's heart was still turned away from God. There've been times during deliverance where people physically encountered the power of God and they still walked away from God or refused to fully commit their lives to Jesus. At the end of the day, the main issue is man's willful sinfulness.

One of the gods Solomon went after was *Chemosh,* the god of the Moabites. Some scholars believe his name meant "destroyer" or "subduer."[59] He was also seen as a fish god, making him a marine spirit.

Marine spirits are also known as anti-marital spirits. I've been able to pray with countless people who would have what they thought random urges to leave their spouses or to be unfaithful to them. After I took them through deliverance and we prayed against the marine spirits, the urges would go.

When you're not married, the devil wants you to do things outside of marriage. When you get married, the devil still wants you to do things outside of marriage. This is truly how marine spirits operate. Their main mission is to destroy God's family model.

Another marine spirit described in the Bible is a giant sea creature known as the Leviathan (Job 3:8, Job 40:25–41:26, Psalm 74:14, Psalm 104:26 and twice in Isaiah 27:1). Isaiah talks about this creature in Isaiah 27, saying, "In that day the Lord with his hard and great and strong sword will punish Leviathan the fleeing serpent, Leviathan the twisting serpent, and he will slay the dragon that is in the sea" (Isaiah 27:1).

On one hand, this passage is talking about Israel's enemies and God destroying them. On the other hand, it's addressing the force behind the enemies attacking Israel, which is Leviathan, the marine spirit that lives in the seas.

> "The leviathan represents the forces of chaos. Of course, this is still no match for the power of God. See Psalms 74. Here God kills the leviathan and gives him as meat to the people in the wilderness…".[60]

Since the meaning of the name Leviathan has to do with twisting, turning, winding, or coiling[61], this marine spirit often brings chaos, and confusion. It twists things and makes it difficult for people to truly understand the truth. When talking to Job about Leviathan, God explained to him how fierce, enormous, and fear provoking this prideful beast was, and how he is king over the sons of pride (Job 40:25-41:26).

Yet Leviathan will have to submit to God! There will come a day where God will punish this demonic entity and cast it into the lake of fire along with all those who were its children. Until then, we must be vigilant and must not allow ourselves to become a part of its children.

So, what are the main doors that let marine spirits into a people's lives? How do we protect ourselves and keep these doors closed? There are four main doors that allow the marine spirits to come into a person's life. The first one is when a family member invites the water demon in through worship. The second door is sexual immorality, and the third is sexual assault. Lastly, the fourth door is when a person invites demonic spirits to live in them.

How do you know if you're dealing with a marine spirit? Well, demons are deceptive, so you can't just assume intellectually that they will always do something a certain way. With this in mind, here are some things that I've seen by taking people with marine spirits through deliverance.

The first thing I've noticed is that a person's manifestation has to do with their physical thirst. I once was with a person outside in broad daylight and I started to talk to her about marine spirits. I explained to her some possible signs for this spirit operating in her life and she looked at me and said, "Oh my gosh, I feel so thirsty." Her whole mouth turned completely dry, like someone who had been in a desert. I immediately took her through deliverance, and when I finished, her mouth visibly changed and she wasn't thirsty anymore.

If people begin to manifest this way, ask them to wait before they drink water. This is very important! If they drink water, marine spirits will get stronger because they will be in their environment. It gives some real context to the term "thirsty", which means that a person is lusting after another person. Some of you may already have felt this unreal thirst for water as you've been reading this book.

Next, encourage the people you are taking through deliverance not to cross their legs. Some people will get an uncontrollable urge to cross their legs. Ask them to please undo their legs because if you don't, it will be near impossible to take them through deliverance. They are worshiping the marine spirit through the crossing of their legs. You may need to command the demonic entities to untie the persons legs if the person has blacked out, which can happen from time to time.

Another sign of a marine spirit is ungovernable crying. The person may look at you during deliverance and say, "I don't know why I'm crying; I just can't stop." That's a marine spirit manifesting. Ask the Holy Spirit to reveal to them the doors that may be open that have brought the marine spirits in. Ask them to repent of any sins, and then command the marine spirits to leave until the person experiences relief.

At times, the person will shed only one tear down one cheek. This may also be marine spirits manifesting. Then have them admit, submit, and resist.

After they resist the devil, command the demons to leave in Jesus' name. Sometimes the marine spirits will work in tandem with spirits of infirmity and cause a multitude of sickness in an individual. We will take a more in-depth look at spirits of infirmity in the coming chapters.

Prayer

> *"Unless the Lord builds the house, those who build it labor in vain. Unless the Lord watches over the city, the watchman stays awake in vain. It is in vain that you rise up early and go late to rest, eating the bread of anxious toil; for he gives to his beloved sleep. Behold, children are a heritage from the Lord, the fruit of the womb a reward. Like arrows in the hand of a warrior are the children of one's youth. Blessed is the man who fills his quiver with them! He shall not be put to shame when he speaks with his enemies in the gate" (Psalm 127:1-5).*

Lord Jesus, please build my house for me! Children are blessing from You and I would like to have children, but my ability to have children is blocked [for the man] /my womb is blocked [for the woman]. Please deliver me from marine spirits! Forgive me for things I did that made me come in agreement with them, and completely, in Jesus' name, deliver me from them!

Chapter 14 Questions

1. What is a marine spirit?

2. What are some passages in Scripture that talk about marine spirits?

3. What are the different things marine spirits do in an individual's life?

4. Who is Egeria and what does she cause?

Chapter 15

JEZEBEL

One of the most infamous people in the Bible is Jezebel. This woman was so vile that you probably won't find her name on the top 100 names to name your daughter. When you look up her name in the dictionary, it is synonymous with a woman who is sexually immoral, morally unrestrained, and a deceiver.

But who was Jezebel? Jezebel was a Phoenician princess whose name originally could have came from the name Baalazebel, which means "Baal has exalted"[62]. The BDB Theological Dictionary defines Jezebel as "unexalted, unmarried, or unhusbanded."

She was the daughter of Ethbaal (Ithobaal I), who was first a priest of Baal before becoming the King of Tyre. Ithobal's name means "with Baal"[63]. The more you get to know Jezebel's origin, the easier it becomes to understand why she was so zealous for Baalism.

Jezebel was a power-hungry murderess who married Ahab, the King of Israel. Ahab was a weak king who allowed Jezebel to lead his kingdom. She was the matriarch of the family. Her actions can be compared to the feminist movement of today that seeks to usurp power and destroy the nuclear family system.

After Ahab married Jezebel, the first thing she did was order the murder of all the prophets of God (1 Kings 18:4,13). She also set up altars, which can be seen as portals, for Baal, which means she gave access to demonic spirits to inhabit the land of Israel. Her influence on the land of Israel was so evil that Jesus would later on describe a woman in the church using the name Jezebel.

> "But I have this against you, that you tolerate that woman Jezebel, who calls herself a prophetess and is teaching and seducing my servants to practice sexual immorality and to eat food sacrificed to idols. I gave her time to repent, but she refuses to repent of her sexual immorality. Behold, I will throw her onto a sickbed, and those who commit adultery with her I will throw into great tribulation, unless they repent of her works, and I will strike her children dead. And all the churches will know that I am he who searches mind and heart, and I will give to each of you according to your works" (Revelation 2:20-23).

In this passage, we can clearly describe the characteristics of the spirit of Jezebel. Number one, people operating under the spirit of Jezebel believe they are God's mouthpiece. Secondly, they teach false doctrines and seduce godly people. Thirdly, they entice people to practice sexual immorality, idolatry, to be adulterous, and be unfaithful to God and His Word.

> "Because of the strong trade guilds in Thyatira, the sexual immorality and the eating of things sacrificed to idols was probably connected with the mandatory social occasions of the guilds. Perhaps a Christian was invited to the monthly meeting of the goldsmith's guild, and the meeting was held at the temple of Apollo. "Jezebel" would allow or encourage

the man to go – perhaps even using a "prophetic" word – and when the man went, he fell into immorality and idolatry…"[64]

What exactly were the guilds? They can be compared to unions today. To be a part of a guild was like a sorority-you had to participate in everything they were doing.

Unfortunately for believers, this meant going to different temples and eating meat sacrificed to idols, committing adultery, and praising the deity that your guild chose to praise. You can already sense the tension this would bring to many believers who would have to choose to not be a part of guild because of the depravity, but in doing so, they wouldn't have good jobs to provide for their families.

Living in this environment had to be difficult enough, and then you add this woman who possibly was in a position of leadership in the church. She was enticing people to compromise their faith and satisfy their fleshly desires. The church at Thyatira really was going through it! But God is a holy God, and He will not allow someone to continually corrupt His church without consequences.

According to Scripture, if the woman with the spirit of Jezebel didn't repent, she was going to be thrown into a sick bed. Similarly, anyone who operates under the influence of the spirit of Jezebel can also be afflicted with sickness if they don't repent. Moreover, those who participate with someone operating in the spirit of Jezebel will get thrown by God into great tribulation.

By this I mean that they too will experience the hardships that Jezebel experienced, and if they still don't repent, then they will die. The children Jesus speaks about has to do with those who were spiritually indoctrinated by her-her followers.

They, too, will face a similar fate as her if they don't repent. What Jesus said them echoes to us today. If you're operating in the spirit of Jezebel, committing adulterous and idolatrous behavior with a Jezebel, or following someone with a Jezebel spirit, repent today and God will show you mercy, grace, and heal you from any spirits of infirmity.

Prayer

Father God, thank you for never leaving me nor forsaking me. I want to repent for teaching false doctrine and listening to false doctrine. Forgive me for operating in a Jezebel spirit and leading people astray. Forgive me for being sexually immoral. Your Word says, "Flee from sexual immorality. Every other sin a person commits is outside the body, but the sexually immoral person sins against his own body" (1 Corinthians 6:18). Because of my sexually immoral behavior and my idolatry, I have opened the door to afflictions. Please heal me, Jesus. Please save me from the terrible decisions I've made. I'm also asking that everyone that I led astray because of my false teachings and awful behavior be restored. Please draw them back to you Lord. In the name of Jesus I pray, amen!

Chapter 15 Questions

1. What are the different meanings for the name Jezebel?

2. If someone calls someone a Jezebel, what are they really saying?

3. What are the different things Jesus says about the woman He called Jezebel in the church of Thyatira?

4. Can you repent for operating as a Jezebel or following someone who is operating in the spirit of Jezebel?

Chapter 16

SPIRITS OF INFIRMITY

~

In the gospel of Luke, Luke tells a story about a lady with a spirit of infirmity. A spirit of infirmity means there was a demonic entity that was causing her sickness. For us to truly understand how Jesus healed her, we need to look at Luke 13:10-17.

> "Now he was teaching in one of the synagogues on the Sabbath. And behold, there was a woman who had had a disabling spirit for eighteen years. She was bent over and could not fully straighten herself. When Jesus saw her, he called her over and said to her, 'Woman, you are freed from your disability.' And he laid his hands on her, and immediately she was made straight, and she glorified God. But the ruler of the synagogue, indignant because Jesus had healed on the Sabbath, said to the people, 'There are six days in which work ought to be done. Come on those days and be healed, and not on the Sabbath day.' Then the Lord answered him, 'You hypocrites! Does not each of you on the Sabbath untie his ox or his donkey from the manger and lead it away to water it? And ought not this woman, a daughter of Abraham whom Satan bound for eighteen years, be loosed from this bond on the Sabbath day?' As he

said these things, all his adversaries were put to shame, and all the people rejoiced at all the glorious things that were done by him."

In the beginning of the passage, we find out that Jesus is teaching in a synagogue, which is a place where believers would congregate. In verse 11, Luke points out that this woman was disabled, but he adds that this disability was due to a demonic spirit that had caused her pain for 18 years!

Jesus, told her, "...Woman, you are freed from your disability." (Luke 13:12) Notice how Jesus did not say "Be healed", but specifically said "freed from your disability". She did not need healing from a natural ailment; she needed deliverance from a demonic onslaught.

Later, in the passage Jesus made a startling revelation. The Pharisees were trying to rebuke Jesus for healing on the Sabbath, and He made this statement, "...ought not this woman, a daughter of Abraham whom Satan bound for eighteen years, be loosed from this bond on the Sabbath day?" (Luke 13:16).

Jesus calls her a daughter of Abraham, a believer, and he accredits the ailment to the devil. This is what's known as a spirit of infirmity: a sickness of any kind brought about from an attack of the devil and his demons.

I want to tell you a true story about a woman of God named Ava who got delivered from a spirit of infirmity in April of 2022. Ava and Todd have known me since before I was saved. When I moved to Cut Bank, Montana in 2014, I got connected with a lady named Teri who took trips to Israel every year and would invite people to come with her.

During our conversation she invited me to go on my first trip to Israel. Since then, I've become a regular attendee on the trips. Wanting others to experience the Holy Land, I reached out to Ava and Todd to see if they wanted come and they agreed.

Our trip was at first scheduled for 2020, but because of the pandemic, none of us were allowed to go. The following year, Israel said that anyone who wanted to come there had to have the vaccine. I was absolutely against it, so I didn't even consider the trip.

However, after talking to Teri and hearing her heart, I realized I never even asked God if I should take the vaccine or not. I called Teri and told her I would pray and get back to her. It was a Friday, and I decided that by Monday I would have an answer for her.

I told my wife about my dilemma and she didn't say much. I spoke to God privately and put out a fleece, seeking out confirmation from God as to whether or not I should be getting the shot. I asked God to give someone else a dream about the situation as a sign.

Saturday morning rolled by and I was discouraged. I was driving by myself and said out loud, "I don't think you're even going to talk to me about this." Suddenly, I got a voice message from a friend who lived in New York City.

I clicked the message and heard my friend Kiki say, "Bro I had a dream about you last night that you took the shot and you ended up on a ventilator. We all were coming into the room in the dream to say goodbye to you."

I could not believe it! I went home quickly and shared the dream with my wife, who said, "I also had a dream along the same line last night. In the dream I was mad at you that you were going to throw your life away over this trip. I was telling you, don't you remember the swine flu and all the adverse reactions people had?"

After hearing this I knew God did not want me personally taking the shot. So I said no to Teri and to going on this free trip to Israel. She was very disappointed and sad. It hurt me to disappoint her, and while I knew I wasn't supposed to go, it was a very painful time.

As things turned out though, Israel didn't allow anyone to come in that year either, so they pushed the trip eventually to the following year, which worked out perfectly for me to go. Ava and her husband Todd flew from Texas and we flew from Montana to New Jersey. From New Jersey, about 39 of us all flew out together to Israel. What a blessing it was to be able to fly again after the whole world was shut down for almost two years!

I was able to connect with Ava and Todd for the first time in years. As we started to talk, Ava began to mention how she was going to get her miracle while she was in Israel. I asked her what was going on and she told me that for the last 15 -18 years, she had been battling rheumatoid arthritis.

I looked at her and said, "You need deliverance. You are demonized". She did not take this to well. She actually just looked at me, smiled a bit, and walked off. The next day during dinner, she and her husband found me and sat at my table. She immediately fired a million questions at me. She was so offended that I would say she was demonized, especially since she had been a church leader for over 25 years and she and her husband had even led Christian marriage counseling for several years as well.

I waited till she was done, then I explained to her that I wasn't saying she had a demon in her spirit, because that is God's throne room. But her soul was fair game, and if she opened the door, the devil was going to come in and cause havoc in her life. After this I stared at her and said, "Do you want to be healed?"

She said yes. She asked if her husband could come for the deliverance session, which I of course agreed to. As soon as we finished eating dinner, I went with them to their hotel room. We were in Bethlehem at the time this took place.

We all walked into the hotel room and I began to explain to her the three prayers that we do: generational, territorial, and personal. She repeated after me and repented for the sins of her forefathers, then we prayed that God would separate her from demonic principalities. She asked for forgiveness for anything she did that connected her to them.

Next, we did personal prayers. She repented for harboring unforgiveness, which is something she told me that she had already been working on. She did not have anything connected to sexual immorality, but she repented for any past things connected to that.

During this time of prayer, she looked at me and said, "I feel like God is telling me to go down on my knees" and she went down by herself. We prayed and then she got up by herself. I remember at that moment that her husband looked like he was about to cry, but I didn't know why at the time.

I then asked the Holy Spirit to reveal to her how many demonic spirits were behind the rheumatoid arthritis. She saw the number 1,000. We asked the Holy Spirit to consolidate, and He brought one main one to the forefront which was fear.

She proclaimed, “There is no fear in love, but perfect love drives out fear, because fear includes punishment, and the one who is afraid has not been perfected in love. We love, because he first loved us” (1 John 4:18-19 LEB). After declaring this and repenting for coming in agreement with fear, I commanded the demonic spirits behind the rheumatoid arthritis to go in Jesus' name!

She felt things leave out of all the places where the pain from the rheumatoid arthritis was-in her chest, her head, her wrist, knees, ankles. Every ache in her body left! To make sure the spirits were all gone, I ran a test. I asked the Holy Spirit to reveal to her if she was healed by making her feet feel heavy, grounded, and rooted in the ground. I looked at her and asked her how her feet felt, and she replied that they felt heavy!

I hugged her and said, “You are healed!” Her husband, with teary eyes, said, “I know she is healed because when she went down by herself and stood up by herself, I knew that she had been healed!” Ava began telling us about how the pain was so bad that she'd always tell her husband that it would be better if she was dead. I looked at her and said, “That's a spirit of death.” She said, “No it's not.” “Yes it is,” I said, and her husband emotionally chimed in, saying, “I've been try to tell her this.”

I told her that she had to renounce all agreement with the spirit of death. I remembered something my friend Jean taught me- that fear is always partnered with death. She repented and we cast out the spirit of death.

She felt it leave her entire being. She then said, “I have all the pills with me that I would take, the ones I was thinking about overdosing on. The sleeping pills and all the other ones I took for the rheumatoid arthritis.” She talked about how she at first was only going to bring some of them, but for whatever reason, she had brought all of them. Her husband and I asked her where the medication was, and she said she had put it in one of her bags. We started looking through all of her bags, and we could not find them. After a little bit, we prayed and asked God to show us where they were. After the prayer, we found them in her backpack.

Todd took them and put them in a plastic bag. Then she went out to the streets of Bethlehem for a walk, and for the first time in a long time, she walked down all those flight of stairs without any pain in her body at all. Todd took her on a long walk, found a garbage can, and tossed her pills in them.

She later said that if Todd did not put them in the garbage can, she was going to try to go find them again, but as soon as he put them in the garbage can she vowed not to touch them.

The next day we went out and traveled everywhere with our guide. We walked through Masada in Israel. We walked up and downstairs; we walked for several miles and she felt no pain whatsoever. The only thing she told me during the day was that she did not sleep the whole night. I looked at her and said, “That’s ok, we may just need to continue to do more deliverance.”

That night when we made it home to our hotel, she fell asleep at 6 pm and woke up at 6 am. She slept better than all of us who all had to deal with jet lag. I later found out that she had allergies so bad that every six months, she would fly to Colorado to get an allergy shot. After our deliverance session, she was healed. Furthermore, she had had a quadruple bypass surgery so her chest had been in pain. All the pain left after the prayer time, and the rheumatoid arthritis never came back!

This healing was not something I did, nor am I special. Jesus came into the room and responded to Ava's sincere faith. This was a real miracle!

After this healing, however, I developed a weird fear of God. For the next two months, I would wake up early in the morning and just think through my life. The thoughts that would go through my mind were, *if God is really this real, what does this mean for my life?*

I begin to repent for living a life of complacency. I, too, was hit that night with the power of God. Her healing was not just for her, but also for me. It started a personal revival in me and made me realize that God was more real than I had ever thought.

I've now seen hundreds of people be healed, and I would say that around 95% of them had a spirit of infirmities. I've now realized many times in the church, we don't see healings because we don't know how to pray.

When somebody comes up to me now seeking healing, I always ask them first and foremost: do you have anybody that you need to forgive? Ninety percent of the time, people tell me they do. After this, I ask them if they're willing to forgive the person/people who hurt them. Nine times out of ten, people agree to. After they forgive the people, I command any spirits of infirmity, if there be any, to leave their body in the name of Jesus.

The most powerful moment after Ava was healed was our trip to Petra. If you've ever been to Petra, you know how vast it is and how far of a walk it is to walk to the top. She decided she was going to attempt this walk. She rode most of the way on a donkey, then she began walking.

At one point she was going to quit, but she pressed on and reached the top. When she did, she whistled a special whistle she and her husband had. He immediately went to where she was and hugged her. (Here is the link to their full testimony https://youtu.be/3Ouh8QuJ4yg)

But what if I had decided to embrace the mentality that most churches have toward deliverance? What would have happened to Ava? Sometimes people are terminally ill, and they need deliverance to get healed!

People need freedom. We cannot just sit back and watch as the world is demonized. WE NEED JESUS TO DELIVER US!

Prayer

> *"Surely he has borne our griefs and carried our sorrows; yet we esteemed him stricken, smitten by God, and afflicted. But he was pierced for our transgressions; he was crushed for our iniquities; upon him was the chastisement that brought us peace, and with his wounds we are healed" (Isaiah 53:4-5).*

Jesus, by your stripes I am healed according to Your Word, but the enemy is reinforcing my affliction. He is causing infirmities to stay in my body. I know, God, that the devil only has as much rights in my body as I give him, so please reveal to me what door I opened that has let this sickness in (if the Lord shows you what door it is, repent for that sin, close the door, and rebuke the spirits of infirmity that came in).

Chapter 16 Questions

1. What's a spirit of infirmity?

2. What passage addresses a spirit of infirmity? Can you find more verses in Scripture that talk about spirits of infirmity and what they are?

3. What does Jesus say to the woman in Luke 13?

Chapter 17

DIVINATION

My friend and I went out to eat one day at a Mongolian restaurant in Great Falls, Montana. As the young female server begin to take our order, I felt like I should invite her to church. So I asked her if she wanted to go to church and she looked at me and said "I'm a witch." "So?" I replied back. She wasn't expecting that response. She looked at me and said, "I'll think about it".

This was a first for me. I'd never had a waitress tell me they were a witch. However, paganism and sorcery are on the rise, especially in the west. I've met countless Christians who have gone to see psychics, and I've come to understand that many believers think that witchcraft can't harm them because they're saved. Thus they dabble in magic games like Dungeons & Dragons, watch shows like Harry Potter, use crystals for energy, go to sun dances, follow new age teachings, practice yoga, astrology, numerology, and reiki, visit medicine men and mediums, and read books full magic.

If we're ignorant, we can open doors to the demonic realm and can come under the influence of witchcraft. Although it's hard to tell if someone is a witch or not, true witches can tell who you are. We can see an example of this in Acts 16.

> "As we were going to the place of prayer, we were met by a slave girl who had a spirit of divination and brought her owners much gain by fortune-telling. She followed Paul and us, crying out, "These men are servants of the Most High God, who proclaim to you the way of salvation." And this she kept doing for many days. Paul, having become greatly annoyed, turned and said to the spirit, "I command you in the name of Jesus Christ to come out of her." And it came out that very hour" (Acts 16:16-18).

There are several things one can learn from this encounter. Number one, the slave girl had a spirit of divination. In Greek, the spirit of divination is *pneuma Pythonos* (πνευμα πυθωνος), which translates to mean "spirit of python". Python was said to be a serpent that lived in Delphi (modern-day southern Greece) and was said to have the power of divination. It's likely that the demon in this slave girl is what the locals knew to be the spirit of Python[65].

Next, there appears to be a clear understanding between the locals in the story and Luke, the writer of the book of Acts, that this spirit of divination came from Gaea, one of the idols they worshipped. This clearly shows once more that idols are not just mere statues.

This slave girl appears to have known that Paul and his friends were men of God. How could this be? I believe the answer is simple: the spirit that operated in her left her body, gathered information, brought it back to her or communicated to other spirits who were in the air, and monitored the men of God.

Demons are master manipulators. You would think that Paul and his friends would be happy that this woman pointed them out as servants of "the" Most High God. Instead, we read that Paul got annoyed and expelled the demon from the slave girl.

He was annoyed because this girl was manipulating the crowd for her own gain. Garnering praise for herself, she was trying to make more money by associating herself with Paul and the other servants of God. Her appeal was springing from error and impure motives.

People who are doing divination are not doing it because the love of God compels them to, no matter how loving they seem. Their motives are impure. Likewise, this slave girl was also doing this to please people instead of pleasing God. This why she announced it so loudly for all to hear. Manipulation seeks people's approval.

Divination, which is also witchcraft, goes hand-in-hand with manipulation. This doesn't mean everyone who struggles with manipulation is a witch but, every witch manipulates. In essence, if one does not deal with their manipulative ways, they can easily fall into divination or be attacked by diviners.

Manipulation can be embedded underneath our thought processes. It flows out of a need for control, and the root of control is fear. It causes people to think of ways we can take advantage of one another instead of outdoing each other in well-doing.

It's important to note that God is never manipulative, He is persuasive. In Greek, the word for faith is *pistis*, which means "divine persuasive trust".

Proverbs 16:21 says, "The wise of heart is called discerning, and sweetness of speech increases persuasiveness". As believers, we should increase persuasion in our speech but never hide manipulation in our love.

Divination is an abomination to God. He makes this clear in Deuteronomy 18, where he says:

> "There shall not be found among you anyone who burns his son or his daughter as an offering, anyone who practices divination or tells fortunes or interprets omens, or a sorcerer or a charmer or a medium or a necromancer or one who inquires of the dead, for whoever does these things is an abomination to the Lord. And because of these abominations the Lord your God is driving them out before you" (Deuteronomy 18:10-12).

If it's an abomination to God, then it should be an abomination to us. As believers we must stop playing with darkness. Like Paul, we must expel every form of divination out of people in Jesus' name!

Prayer

Father in Heaven, I bless Your name! Lord, I ask for forgiveness. Forgive me for participating in witchcraft. Forgive me for being manipulative. Forgive me for rebelling against Your ways and pursuing my own motives. I also ask that any curse that has been spoken over me by family members or any diviners be broken in Jesus' name!

Jesus, Your Word says, "Like a fluttering sparrow or a darting swallow, an undeserved curse does not come to rest" (Proverbs 26:2 NIV). If there are things, Holy Spirit, that I did or that my family did that has caused curses to rest on me, please, Jesus, reveal them to me. I repent for those doors that I have opened in my life through things I did or my family did. I also pray against any curses the diviners have done over my city and my country. I pray in Jesus' name that your fire would consume any evil altar that those who are practicing the dark arts have built. I tear down their strongholds in Jesus' name! Amen!

Chapter 17 Questions

1. What does the word *divination* mean in Greek?

2. What's the emphasis the author makes about idols and why does he make it?

3. What does the author believe goes hand-in-hand with witchcraft?

4. What doesn't God ever do?

Chapter 18

THE ARMOR OF GOD

After explaining what our true struggle is against, Paul tells us how to defeat these demonic entities. Within these valuable truths, Paul discusses the blueprint for how to maintain one's freedom and help others receive theirs as well. Paul writes,

> "Therefore put on the full armor of God, so that when the day of evil comes, you may be able to stand your ground, and after you have done everything, to stand. Stand firm then, with the belt of truth buckled around your waist, with the breastplate of righteousness in place, and with your feet fitted with the readiness that comes from the gospel of peace. In addition to all this, take up the shield of faith, with which you can extinguish all the flaming arrows of the evil one. Take the helmet of salvation and the sword of the Spirit, which is the word of God. And pray in the Spirit on all occasions with all kinds of prayers and requests. With this in mind, be alert and always keep on praying for all the Lord's people" (Ephesians 6:13-18 NIV).

As Paul continues to explain the battle we're in, he says, "therefore put on the full armor of God, so that when the day of evil comes". As believers, if we want to maintain our freedom, we must first realize that we can't have just some of the armor of God on. We must put all of it on because the day of evil is inevitable.

The term *day* is not just referencing a single day, but rather an array of days. The saying *day of evil* refers to spiritual attacks. The next thing a person must do to continue walking freely is be prepared for spiritual attacks. Freedom is not lack of awareness, nor is it a lack of readiness. It is preparation in every occasion; knowledge that we must defend what is ours.

We cannot simply pray the day of evil (spiritual attacks) will never come, for every believer will be spiritually attacked. One example of a spiritual attack is persecution. Jesus says this about persecution, "Remember the word that I said to you: 'A slave is not greater than his master.' If they persecuted me, they will also persecute you. If they kept my word, they will keep yours also" (John 15:20 LEB).

We can be ready for spiritual attacks as we pray. A good reminder for everyone who goes through deliverance is that deliverance is ongoing. When a person is delivered from one area, the enemy finds another way to attack. This is why Jesus taught His disciples to pray, "lead us not unto temptation, but deliver us from the evil one" (Matthew 6:13).

God does not tempt anyone, so we should never think He is the one leading us into temptation (James 1:13). Rather, God will try us, test us, and still in His goodness offer us a way out of the test. Pray that you will not be led into the test.

Jesus also teaches them to pray, "but deliver us from the evil one." Notice how these are not unbelievers who need deliverance, but those who are disciples of Jesus. Jesus never tells them to pray that they would never experience evil or the evil one, but that they would be rescued from the evil. This should be our expectation going into battle. If you come into a fight thinking the wrong way, then you've already lost the fight.

Understand, therefore, that you're in a spiritual war. This spiritual war will not end until the day Jesus comes back. The armor of God is to ready you for the battle and to help you win, but it won't prevent you from experiencing it.

In Ephesians 6:13, Paul says, *"...you may be* able to stand your ground, *and after you have done everything to stand (Ephesians 6:13).* To stay free, a believer must stand their ground. This means we can't quit or go backwards, no matter how grim the situation looks (Luke 9:62).

When the children of Israel were stuck between the Red Sea and Pharaoh and his army, Moses told them,

> "...Do not be afraid. Stand firm and you will see the deliverance the Lord will bring you today. The Egyptians you see today you will never see again. The Lord will fight for you; you need only to be still" (Exodus 14:13-14 NIV).

Similarly, Paul tells the church in Ephesus to stand, although the spiritual attacks may seem overwhelming, the verse continues on, with Paul saying, "Stand firm then, with the belt of truth buckled around your waist, with the breastplate of righteousness in place" (Ephesians 6:14 NIV). What is the belt of truth? Why does it have to be put on first?

During the time Paul wrote this letter, Israel was under Roman occupation. The Romans had the greatest army at this time, and their armor played a major role in their successful conquests. Paul was using imagery that connected the Roman armor to the armor of God. The belt was an essential part of this armor. It kept all the under garments in place. As one commentary puts it,

> "It was the belt that held the scabbard, without which there would be no place to put a sword. Imagine an overzealous soldier, fired up and charging out into battle—but without his belt, and consequently without a weapon!"[66]

Likewise, we as believers must have truth fastened securely around our waist. It must be what holds our "garments" (our thoughts, our lives) together. The belt being girded was also a sign that the soldier was prepared and ready for whatever may come.

> "Let your loins be girded about, and your lights burning; and ye yourselves like unto men that wait for their Lord, when he will return from the wedding; that when he cometh and knocketh, they may open unto him immediately. Blessed are those servants, whom the Lord when he cometh shall find watching: verily I say unto you, that he shall gird himself, and make them to sit down to meat, and will come forth and serve them. And if he shall come in the second watch, or come in the third watch, and find them so, blessed are those servants" (Luke 12:35-38 KJV).

The truth of God keeps us awake and alert. When deception arises, we will not be overcome by it because we are securely held by the truth of God's Word. A demon is just a side effect; the real issue is the lie a person believes. It's the root of the problem. Truth always overcomes lies. The belt of truth helps us rightly understand the weapons we need to use and how and when to use them.

Next, Paul told the church in Ephesus to put on the *breastplate of righteousness* (Ephesians 6:14). This part of the armor has to do with our position in Christ. Christ Himself has positioned us, and our righteousness is not merited but inherited through His work on the cross. As Scripture says, "For our sake he made him to be sin who knew no sin, so that in him we might become the righteousness of God" (2 Corinthians 5:21).

The breastplate of righteousness guards one of the most important parts of your body, which is your heart. The Bible says, "Above all else, guard your heart, for everything you do flows from it" (Proverbs 4:23 NIV). There is no greater way to guard your heart than for you to allow God to have full residency in it.

Paul then discusses another part of the armor that helps us walk in peace, and these are the sandals (which represent the gospel of peace). It's important to note that they are fitted. Have you ever worn the wrong size of shoes? If they're too big, you stumble and fall over your own feet. If they're too small, you will experience pain and agony.

This teaches us that the gospel is not meant for us to live vicariously through others. It must be between us and God first, and we must walk it out.

Gospel means the *greatest* news! We were dead in our trespasses, but God, who is full of mercy, sent his son, Jesus. Although Jesus was sinless, He became sin so that all who believe in Him would no longer have to die for their sins. He has brought us peace!

One of the greatest weapons we have against all the powers of darkness is the fact that we're at peace with God. The war that Gideon and the Israelites fought in the book of Judges was secondary to them not being at peace with God. When the angel of the Lord first appeared to Gideon, he didn't know who it was. However, after the angel of the Lord consumed Gideon's food with fire and went up to heaven in the same flame, Gideon became afraid.

God proclaimed to them, "Peace be with you. Do not fear; you will not die". At that moment, the true war inside subsided.

> "And Gideon realized that he was the angel of Yahweh; and Gideon said, "Oh, my Lord Yahweh! For now I have seen the angel of Yahweh face to face" (Judges 6:22 LEB). But what was Gods response amidst his fears? "And Yahweh said to him, "Peace be with you. Do not fear; you will not die"' (Judges 6:23 LEB).

Gideon was able to build an altar and call it *Yahweh is Peace* (Yahweh Shalom). This is the only place in the Bible this name for God is found. None of his enemies were destroyed yet, but he could still be at peace knowing God was at peace with him.

> "For he himself is our peace, who made both one and broke down the dividing wall of the partition, the enmity, in his flesh, invalidating the law of commandments in ordinances, in order that he might create the

> two in himself into one new man, thus making peace, and might reconcile both in one body to God through the cross, killing the enmity in himself. And coming, he proclaimed the good news of peace to you who were far away and peace to the ones who were near" (Ephesians 2:14-17 LEB).

What, then, is our responsibility? We must share the great news with others (thus the gospel sandals). For the Bible states,

> "How beautiful upon the mountains are the feet of him who brings good news, who publishes peace, who brings good news of happiness, who publishes salvation, who says to Zion, "Your God reigns"' (Isaiah 52:7).

Another part of the armor that helps support our freedom is the shield of faith. Paul says, "In addition to all this, take up the shield of faith, with which you can extinguish all the flaming arrows of the evil one" (Ephesians 6:16 NIV). Faith combats doubt.

How does faith come? Romans 10:17 says that "faith comes from hearing, and hearing through the word of Christ" (Romans 10:17). When a person spends time with Christ by listening to and reading His Word, faith will come.

> "He did not weaken in faith when he considered his own body, which was as good as dead (since he was about a hundred years old), or when he considered the barrenness of Sarah's womb. No unbelief made him waver concerning the promise of God, but he grew strong in his faith as he gave glory to God, "fully convinced that God was able to do what he had promised" (Romans 4:21).

Abraham's faith grew stronger as he gave God glory. When we give thanksgiving, we gain greater confidence in God. This should cause us to be fully convinced that if God decrees anything, it will be done! So faith comes through the Word of Christ, but it grows stronger as we praise God during trials.

The Bible says that the shield of faith is meant to extinguish all the flaming arrows of the devil. One example of Satan's flaming arrows is fear. Fear is the devil's faith.

> "There is no fear in love, but perfect love casts out fear. For fear has to do with punishment, and whoever fears has not been perfected in love" (1 John 4:18).

This is why we need the full armor. We need to keep this verse securely around our waist, as it will keep our thoughts together. When you read it and know it's the truth, you can have faith and trust that God loves you perfectly. As you believe this truth, the fiery arrows of fear are extinguished.

Another thing we must put on is the helmet of salvation (Ephesians 6:17). The helmet of salvation has to do with the hope of salvation and deliverance from thoughts that attempt to invade your mind.

> "But since we belong to the day, let us be sober, putting on faith and love as a breastplate, and the hope of salvation as a helmet. For God did not appoint us to suffer wrath but to receive salvation through our Lord Jesus Christ" (1 Thessalonians 5:8-9 NIV).

As believers, we must know that God will never leave us. We may choose to walk away from God, but our faith should not be on what we can do, but on God's faithfulness. The enemy wants us to question our salvation. While it's important for us to examine our hearts and see if we're in the faith, this is not the type of questioning the enemy wants us to do. He wants us to question the validity and ability of truth.

The second thing the helmet of salvation does is deliver us from the invasive thoughts the enemy brings to our minds. The devil knows that if he can control our thoughts, he can cause us to act how he wants us to. The Word of God tells us, "We destroy arguments and every lofty opinion raised against the knowledge of God, and take every thought captive to obey Christ," (2 Corinthians 10:5).

We who are saved have been given the authority to take thoughts that don't glorify God, rebuke them in Jesus' name, and retrain our thinking by meditating on the Word of God! If we are saved, then we shouldn't think as orphans but as children of God. We have to be confident in Christ that He is able to keep us (Jude 1:24).

Along with the helmet of salvation, another thing that helps us stay grounded in our freedom is the sword of the Spirit, which is the Word of God (Ephesians 6:17). This refers to the sword of the Holy Spirit. On this topic, the Enduring Word Commentary states,

> "The idea is that the *Spirit provides a sword* for you, and that *sword is the word of God.* To effectively use the sword of the Spirit, we can't regard the Bible as a book of magic charms or tie one around our neck the way that garlic is said to drive away vampires. To effectively use the

sword, we must regard it as the word of God – *which is the word of God*. If we are not confident in the inspiration of Scripture, that the sword really came from the Spirit, then we will not use it effectively at all".[67]

The word used for *word* in this passage is *rhema*, which refers to something that has been spoken by a living person. The other Greek word for *word* is *logos*, which means the constant written Word (John 1:1).

Therefore, we use the Word of God as a sword by speaking it out under the inspiration and direction of the Holy Spirit. So, when we're meditating on God's Word, we are filling our gun with spiritual ammunition and the Holy Spirit, through prayer, teaches us how to fire it!

Next, a person who wants to walk in their freedom must have a prayer life. Paul says, "praying at all times in the Spirit, with all prayer and supplication. To that end, keep alert with all perseverance, making supplication for all the saints," (Ephesians 6:18).

The first type of prayer he mentions is the *prayer in the spirit*, which refers to praying in the Holy Spirit. It's a great weapon against the enemy because praying in the Spirit helps us become a witness for Jesus (Acts 1:8), builds up our inner being (1 Corinthians 14:4), and helps us pray the perfect will of God (Romans 8:26).

Next, the verse discusses it says, "all prayers and supplications". By *all prayers,* it's saying,

"We should use every kind of prayer we can think of. Group prayer, individual prayer, silent prayer, shouting prayer, walking prayer, kneeling prayer, eloquent prayer, groaning prayer, constant prayer, fervent prayer – *just pray*"[68].

This also connects to the four types of prayers found in 1 Timothy 2:1-4: supplications, prayers, intercessions, and thanksgiving. The sword of the Spirit, which is the Word of God, should be utilized in prayer. I'd say there are two ways to properly use the Word of God: through preaching it and through praying it!

The final steps to keeping our freedom are these three things: keeping alert, persevering, and praying for others. First, we must keep alert. The Bible tells us to, "be sober-minded; be watchful. [Our] adversary the devil prowls around like a roaring lion, seeking someone to devour" (1 Peter 5:8). Being sober-minded is the same as being alert, which means not falling asleep or getting complacent. When we do, the enemy can devour us.

Next is perseverance, which is built through trials. It helps shape our character and deepens our well of hope.

> "Not only so, but we also glory in our sufferings, because we know that suffering produces perseverance; perseverance, character; and character, hope. And hope does not put us to shame, because God's love has been poured out into our hearts through the Holy Spirit, who has been given to us" (Romans 5:3-5 NIV).

Lastly, we must pray for others. When we focus on ourselves, we can become selfish and become a home for demons. James 3:16 says, "For where you have envy and selfish ambition, there you find disorder and every evil practice" (James 3:16 NIV). As we pray for others, it helps us focus less on ourselves and it teaches us the heart of God. If God has set you free, it's time for you to pray that others will experience freedom as well!

Prayer

Jesus, please teach me how to maintain my freedom! Break the cycles of sin off of my life! I put the belt of truth around my waist so I can be grounded in truth. I put on the breastplate of righteousness. I'm made righteous through Jesus Christ. I put on the fitted gospel of peace shoes that You have given me. I grab the shield of faith and I extinguish the arrows of the enemy. For my mind, I put on the helmet of salvation. I also grab the sword of the Spirit, which is the Word of God, and I declare it out in Jesus' name! Jesus, I clothe myself with the armor of the Spirit. Please help me to maintain my freedom and help me to liberate others who are in bondage in the mighty name of Jesus!

Your Word says, "Rescue those being led away to death; hold back those staggering toward slaughter. If you say, 'But we knew nothing about this,' does not he who weighs the heart perceive it? Does not he who guards your life know it? (Proverbs 24:11-12 NIV).

Help me to snatch people out of hell fire (Jude 1:22-23). Thank you for freeing me, Jesus. I know that You are able "to keep [me] from stumbling and to present [me] blameless before the presence of [Your] glory with great joy," (Jude 1:24).

Chapter 18 Questions

1. What is the armor of God?

2. According to the author, what does the armor of God help a believer do?

3. What are the different parts of the armor of God and what is the significance of each of them?

Chapter 19

GENERATIONAL CURSES

~~~

During my struggle with pornography, a prophetess came to me and said, "what your grandparents refused to deal with, and your parents did not kill, you are left to destroy." I knew she was speaking about my addiction to pornography, and the words she spoke to me helped reassure that I would be free. It made me realize that this did not start with me, but it would finish with me!

In the book of Leviticus, God spoke to the children of Israel and told them that only through confessing their sins and the sins of their forefathers would God fully forgive them, heal their land, and remember His covenant that He had made.

> "But if they will confess their sins and the sins of their ancestors—their unfaithfulness and their hostility toward me, which made me hostile toward them so that I sent them into the land of their enemies—then when their uncircumcised hearts are humbled and they pay for their sin, I will remember my covenant with Jacob and my covenant with Isaac and my covenant with Abraham, and I will remember the land" (Leviticus 26:40-42 NIV).
~~~

I've found that many Christians, especially in western culture, don't believe in generational curses. Many don't believe that generational curses can still exist for believers.

Let's say a person goes to the doctors and the doctor asks "Did your grandma have heart problems"? And they say "Yes." Then the doctor would ask, "Did your mom have heart problems?", and if the person responds, "Yes," what do you believe the doctor will check for in this individual? Heart problems.

Why would the doctors check if the individual has heart problems? It's because genetically, things get passed down from our parents. This is why if you have alcoholism in your family, you should avoid drinking alcohol because you're at a high risk. The same goes for cancer, mental illness, sexual immorality, afflictions, behavioral patterns from our families, and even inherited trauma.

> "Intergenerational trauma is the theory that trauma can be inherited because there are genetic changes in a person's DNA. The changes from trauma do not damage the gene (genetic change). Instead, they alter how the gene functions (epigenetic change)"[69].

We can also get a good picture of a generational curse by looking at the story of Abraham and Sarah. In this story, Sarah is barren. After years of praying, God answered their prayers and Isaac was born (Genesis 21:1-7). When Isaac was 40 years old, he married Rebekah, who was the granddaughter of Abraham's brother Nahor. The Bible says that she was barren, and Isaac pleaded with God on her behalf. Twenty years later, she bore her children[70].

"Now Isaac pleaded with the Lord for his wife, because she was barren; and the Lord granted his plea, and Rebekah his wife conceived" (Genesis 25:21 NKJV).

The word *pleaded* (also sometimes translated "entreated") means he supplicated to God on a regular basis, crying out to Him nonstop. The faith of the fathers affects their children! I'm sure Isaac heard of his birth story from his parents repeatedly. I can imagine that he was greatly influenced by it and that it produced a greater faith in him, for his faith did not waver at all.

Rebekah gave birth to twins, Esau and Jacob. Jacob stole his brother's birthright and was sent to his mother's side of the family to get a wife (Genesis 25-29). While at Laban's home, he fell in love with Rachel, Laban's younger daughter.

Laban deceived Jacob. Having promised Jacob that he could marry Rachel, he deceitfully gave him Leah instead on his wedding night. So instead of one wife, Jacob ended up with two.

The question is, which one of these two wives was barren? Many people always say Rachel, but the real answer is both. The Bible says, "When the Lord saw that Leah was unloved, He opened her womb; but Rachel was barren" (Genesis 29:31 NKJV).

We later read that God remembered Rachel. He "listened to her and opened her womb" (Genesis 30:22 NKJV). We can then ask the question, whose side is this barrenness coming from?

Since Sarah was Abraham's half-sister (Genesis 20:12) and all of his children and grandchildren married into his family, it seems reasonable to conclude that something in Abraham's line affected the women in his family. This is one of the ways a generational curse works.

Abraham's family also had a generational lying problem. Twice Abraham told a half-truth and said Sarah was his sister, leaving out the fact that she was also his wife (Genesis 12:18-20; 20:12). Sarah lied to God about laughing (Genesis 18:15) and Isaac lied and said Rebekah was his sister when they were really second cousins (Genesis 26:1-16).

Isaac and Rebekah give birth to a child who was known as a deceiver (Genesis 27:36). Rebekah helped Jacob lie to her father so he could steal the birthright. Jacob, in turn, gave birth to ten liars who sold their brother and lied to their father about it (Genesis 37:31-32). If we do not stop generational sins, they will only grow worse throughout our bloodline and could end up destroying our lineage.

Chapter 20

DELIVERANCE PRAYERS

~~~

The most effective way to pray is to follow the leading of the Holy Spirit. These prayer steps are meant to give you a starting point. To reiterate, the three sets of prayers are generational, territorial, and personal.

When you begin to pray, remember to make sure you pray over any liquid you use. If you're praying for yourself, don't drink any liquid until you're done. If you're praying for someone, ask them not to drink any liquid until you're finished praying against marine spirits. Also, make sure nobody's legs are crossed during deliverance.

When doing a full session of deliverance, I highly encourage you to fast and pray prior to it. Please do not take someone through deliverance by yourself (unless it's your spouse). Always try to have a partner with you. Pray these next prayers for yourself, or if you're taking someone through deliverance, have them repeat after you.

- I stand with my ancestors to ask for forgiveness for every evil altar we may have built, every sexual immorality we have committed, any
~~~

innocent blood we have shed, for breaking the Ten Commandments, and for sins we did knowingly and unknowingly. Please forgive us.

This prayer can be likened to the prayer that Daniel prayed in Daniel 9 when he would repeatedly say "we" have sinned. Daniel was one of the most righteous people on the earth (Ezekiel 14:14), yet he humbles himself and includes himself in the sins of all of the nation of Israel, past and present.

Demonic territorial spirits

- Lord, please disconnect me from every demonic territorial spirit, demonic principality, authority, the cosmic powers over this present darkness, and the spiritual forces of evil in the heavenly places (Ephesians 6:12).

Personal

- Jesus, forgive (me or us) for harboring bitterness and unforgiveness towards (<u>have them name everyone the Holy Spirit places on their heart</u>). Please take out of me every demonic spirit that came into me because of me harboring bitterness and unforgiveness.

Next, say, "Please let me pray for you now" (or you can start praying over yourself). Let them know they can close their eyes if they want.

Ask them to let you know when they sense things going on in their body like: lightness, weight lifting off of them, clarity of mind, headaches, heart aches, pain in random or specific places, or irrational or evil thoughts. If any of these things and/or anything that resembles this starts happening, ask them to let you know by nodding their head up and down.

Now say, "I command every demonic spirit that came in through unforgiveness to come out in Jesus' name!" Repeat the phrase, "Come out in Jesus' name" until either you sense the spirit lift off them or they feel it.

Sexual Immorality

Tell them to repeat after you. Say, "Jesus, please forgive me for being sexually immoral. Please take out of me every demonic spirit that came into my life through me being sexually immoral."

Then say, "Let me pray for you."

"I command every demonic spirit that came into ____________ through sexual immorality to come out in Jesus' name! Continue to repeat "Come out in Jesus' name" until they feel something lift off of them. When they do, ask, "Where did you feel it lift from?"

If anyone has experienced sexual abuse, someone in their generation praying to water demons, sex outside of marriage, any type of sexual sin including watching pornography, worshipping spirits in the water or gods that are marine spirits, that person likely has marine spirits.

You must now at this point have the Holy Spirit help you expose them. These demons like to hide, and they believe the individuals whom they capture are their spouses. Take some anointing oil, place it on their ring finger, and have them repent of all sexual immorality. Ask them to pray that Jesus would issue a decree of divorce with all the marine spirits that believe the individual is their spouse.

Then ask the Holy Spirit to reveal to them how many marine spirits have come into them through them being sexually immoral, sexual immorality in their genealogy, or any ancestral worship of water demons. Ask them to listen to the voice of the Holy Spirit and explain to them that they will either hear a number, see a number, or know the number. Keep asking the Holy Spirit to reveal it. Be persistent (Luke 11:5-13).

After this persistent prayer (some people who are sensitive to hearing the voice of the Holy Spirit may get the number before you even ask), ask them what number they got. If it's a high number like 1,000, ask the Holy Spirit to consolidate the number for you, bring the main ones or one to the forefront, and give them a new number. Whatever number they get now, work with it (unless of course the Holy Spirit tells you it's not correct. This is why discernment is needed here).

After you receive this consolidated number, ask for the leader. Since there are hierarchies in the demonic kingdom, you need to first deal with the leader. Ask the Holy Spirit to reveal to them the name of the leader of these marine spirits (Luke 8:30). They will most likely get a name. Sometimes, it will be the exact name of the entity, while other times it will be a name the demonic entity is associated with, either through using that person in a vile way or attacking them. Moreover, the name also may be a sin the person or the person's family is dealing with.

For this example, they may see or hear the name, "Lust". After this, you would need to find out what the assignment is. John 10:10 tells us that "the thief comes only to steal and kill and destroy. I came that they may have life and have it abundantly". The assignment will be connected to stealing, killing, or destroying. For example, the person may say something like, "Kill my dreams".

It's important to write this down. Then you'll ask the individual what door that allowed the leader "Lust" to come in. The Bible says,

> "Do not love the world or the things in the world. If anyone loves the world, the love of the Father is not in him. For all that is in the world—the desires of the flesh and the desires of the eyes and pride of life—is not from the Father but is from the world. And the world is passing away along with its desires, but whoever does the will of God abides forever" (1 John 2:15-17).

Open doors will most likely come from these three things: lust of the flesh, desires of the eyes, and the pride of life. The person may then answer you and say something like, "I see a candy that I stole when I was four years old." Ask them to repent for stealing the candy, and then counter the assignment that the demonic entity had for them with the truth of God's Word.

> "For I know the plans I have for you, declares the Lord, plans for welfare and not for evil, to give you a future and a hope. Then you will call upon me and come and pray to me, and I will hear you. You will seek me and find me, when you seek me with all your heart" (Jeremiah 29:11-13).

Pray that every consequence would be nullified in Jesus name!

Last but not least, command the leader to completely go in Jesus' name. Repeat, "Come out in Jesus' name" persistently until they feel a release and ask them where they felt the spirit leave from. You ask this because sometimes these beings are connected to pain that the person may have been feeling in their bodies for a long time, and where they leave or how they leave can be a sign of these infirmities.

Then ask the Holy Spirit to again reveal to them how many marine spirits are left after the leader has been expelled. For whatever number they give you, repeat the process of what you did for the leader. Address the next in line and get their name, assignment, and the door they came through. Do this until all of them are completely gone.

During this time, people who are barren or have had miscarriages often experience breakthrough, and many others will have kids again without any complications.

Now you backtrack a bit and deal with the territorial demonic spirits. Pray that Jesus would disconnect the person or people from: principalities, authorities, cosmic powers over this present darkness, and the forces of evil in heavenly places. Cast them out like you did the other spirits. Command them to leave in Jesus' name until you and/or the person you're taking through deliverance feels a release.

Next, deal with demonic spirits that came in generationally. Say, "I'm going to ask the Holy Spirit to reveal to you how many demonic spirits have come generationally into your life. You're going to get a number, and when you do, please let me know what it is". After they get the number, find out the name, assignment, and the door. Do the same thing you did for the marine spirits.

Note: not everyone will know how to freely allow the Holy Spirit to speak to them. With this in mind, if they can't get the name, then just focus on the generational lies they believe that have caused them to be bound. You can ask something like, "Holy Spirit, please reveal to them how many lies of the enemy have come in generationally that are keeping them bound."

Ask them if the Holy Spirit has brought a number to their mind. For whatever number they have, there will be a leader or a general. Since demons have ranks, if you don't deal with the leader of a military group, the militants will come back.

This is why it's important to isolate the leader. You do this by asking the Holy Spirit to reveal the main lie that keeps all other lies there. The person you are praying for may hear the Holy Spirit say something like, "I will never amount to anything."

Since this lie has to do with their purpose, you would then pull out the sword of the Spirit (the Word of God) and find a verse that speaks about purpose (thank God for internet access on our phones!). Have them declare in first person, "For [I] am his workmanship, created in Christ Jesus for good works, which God prepared beforehand, that [I] should walk in them" (Ephesians 2:10).

Combat the lie with the truth of God's Word. Then, cast out the demonic spirit associated with that lie and all those underneath it. Command it to leave until the person senses a release or the Holy Spirit tells you to stop.

Ask them afterward if they heard, felt, or sensed anything. Most likely, they'll say yes and tell you what they sensed. Occasionally, individuals may not sense anything. If need be, ask Holy Spirit to reveal to them what is hindering them from hearing His voice, and have them proclaim a verse that declares sonship and gives them the right as a child to hear the Father's voice.

Ask the Holy Spirit to reveal to them how many more lies are left and repeat the process. Start with the leader and command it and all those under it to leave until all of them are gone.

Chapter 21

SIX IMPORTANT FACTS ON DELIVERANCE

1. There is power in the name of Jesus.

   "And being found in human form, he humbled himself by becoming obedient to the point of death, even death on a cross. Therefore God has highly exalted him and bestowed on him the name that is above every name, so that at the name of Jesus every knee should bow, in heaven and on earth and under the earth, and every tongue confess that Jesus Christ is Lord, to the glory of God the Father" (Philippians 2:8-11).

2. God's Word must be foundational.

   "For the word of God is living and active, sharper than any two-edged sword, piercing to the division of soul and of spirit, of joints and of marrow, and discerning the thoughts and intentions of the heart. And no creature is hidden from his sight, but all are naked and exposed to the eyes of him to whom we must give account" (Hebrews 4:12-13).

3. The Spirit of God must lead. Methodologies are only there to help form structure, but the ultimate leader must be the Spirit of God.

"Nevertheless, I tell you the truth: it is to your advantage that I go away, for if I do not go away, the Helper will not come to you. But if I go, I will send him to you. And when he comes, he will convict the world concerning sin and righteousness and judgment: concerning sin, because they do not believe in me; concerning righteousness, because I go to the Father, and you will see me no longer; concerning judgment, because the ruler of this world is judged. "I still have many things to say to you, but you cannot bear them now. When the Spirit of truth comes, he will guide you into all the truth, for he will not speak on his own authority, but whatever he hears he will speak, and he will declare to you the things that are to come. He will glorify me, for he will take what is mine and declare it to you" (John 16:7-14).

4. There is no room for the wisdom of man. When you are doing deliverance all your wisdom must remain submitted to the Spirit. "And I, when I came to you, brothers, did not come proclaiming to you the testimony of God with lofty speech or wisdom. For I decided to know nothing among you except Jesus Christ and him crucified. And I was with you in weakness and in fear and much trembling, and my speech and my message were not in plausible words of wisdom, but in demonstration of the Spirit and of power, so that your faith might not rest in the wisdom of men but in the power of God" (1 Corinthians 2:1-5).

5. There is no room for pride. We don't know more than God. Just because we don't understand something doesn't mean it's not real. If

you want to understand everything before you trust God, then you might struggle with deliverance.

"But he gives more grace. Therefore it says, 'God opposes the proud but gives grace to the humble'" (James 4:6).

6. Living an intimate life with Jesus is of the utmost importance for someone who wants to do deliverance.

   "And God was doing extraordinary miracles by the hands of Paul, so that even handkerchiefs or aprons that had touched his skin were carried away to the sick, and their diseases left them and the evil spirits came out of them. Then some of the itinerant Jewish exorcists undertook to invoke the name of the Lord Jesus over those who had evil spirits, saying, "I adjure you by the Jesus whom Paul proclaims." Seven sons of a Jewish high priest named Sceva were doing this. But the evil spirit answered them, "Jesus I know, and Paul I recognize, but who are you?" And the man in whom was the evil spirit leaped on them, mastered all of them and overpowered them, so that they fled out of that house naked and wounded" (Acts 19:11-16).

Chapter 22

ITEMS & PRACTICES THAT OPEN DOORS

~~~

I've included in this chapter is a list of things that can open doors to demonic activity in your life. This is not a list to judge others or yourself, but to help examine the heart. Be kind, gentle, and gracious with those who are breaking ties with the demonic and the things of this world.

> "Do not love the world or the things in the world. If anyone loves the world, the love of the Father is not in him. For all that is in the world—the desires of the flesh and the desires of the eyes and pride of life—is not from the Father but is from the world. And the world is passing away along with its desires, but whoever does the will of God abides forever" (1 John 2:15-17).

Items and practices that open doors:

- Crystals used for energy or received from demonic rituals
- Evil tattoos such as tattoos of the dead/ having tattoos with names of dead loved ones or of dead things.
~~~

You shall not make any cuttings in your flesh for the dead, nor tattoo any marks on you: I am the LORD (Leviticus 19:28 NKJV).

- Tattoos you've gotten through rebellion or wrong motives (I don't believe all tattoos are evil. We are in the New Covenant, but where, how, what, and why matters when you are getting a tattoo).
- Marijuana
- DMT's
- Cigarettes/vaping
- Astro-projecting
- Remote healing
- Reiki healing
- Unbiblical meditations
- False religion
- Abortion
- New Age beliefs
- Meditative yoga
- Yoga
- Tantra
- Kundalini
- Energy
- Idols
- Gematria
- Cult and occultist practices
- Celebrating some holidays (such as the day of the dead). I do not celebrate Halloween nor encourage others to do so. However, I believe it can be used to reach the lost if there is intentionality. I do not condone those who shame people who want to celebrate Halloween.
- Demonic special knowledge
- Mysticisms

- Mormonism
- Islam
- Ouija boards
- 8 Balls
- Frequencies
- Crystal balls
- Incense used for meditation and pursuit of other deities.
- Good luck charms
- Sage
- Pendulums
- Tarot cards
- Angel readings
- Erotica
- Chakras books
- Numerology
- Manifestations
- The Law of Attraction (different from reaping what you sow)
- Twin flame connection
- Vows or promises made that were not kept or done outside of God
- Energy
- False gods
- Talisman
- Astrology reading
- Psychics
- Paraphernalia
- Homosexuality
- Lesbianism
- Gender dysphoria
- Praying to saints or angels

- Sun dances
- Addictions that don't glorify God
- Anal sex in the marriage
- Cowardice
- Unclean books
- Unclean DVDs/shows
- Using sex toys outside of marriage
- Dream catchers
- Clothing (with demonic images on them or received from individuals who are practicing witchcraft)
- Journal/laptop (that has been used for evil)
- Plaque with Mary and child
- Crucifix with Jesus on it
- Stuffed animals (if the Spirit leads or if it's given from someone using witchcraft)
- Ungodly rock and rap music
- Some conspiracy theories
- Pharmaceuticals (drugs/medicines taken without consulting the Lord and your doctor)

"Now the works of the flesh are evident: sexual immorality, impurity, sensuality, idolatry, sorcery, enmity, strife, jealousy, fits of anger, rivalries, dissensions, divisions, envy, drunkenness, orgies, and things like these. I warn you, as I warned you before, that those who do such things will not inherit the kingdom of God" (Galatians 5:19-21).

- Pride
- Fairies
- Marine spirits (mermaids & mermen)

- Gnome/Dwarf/Goblin
- Elves
- Ghosts and Apparitions

Jesus told the disciples, “Behold, I have given you authority to tread on serpents and scorpions, and over all the power of the enemy, and nothing shall hurt you” (Luke 10:19). By snakes and scorpions, Jesus meant demonic entities. The same authority that was given to the apostles, then, has been given to us now, and we can, as David said, “bring [souls] out of prison, that [they] may praise [His] name” (Psalms 142:7 NKJV) through the liberating process of deliverance.

References

1. Strong's greek: 4991. σωτηρία (sótéria) -- deliverance, salvation. Accessed May 21, 2023. https://biblehub.com/greek/4991.htm.

2. November 01, 2020 by Kingdom Works Studios https://conquerseries.com/15-mind-blowing-statistics-about-pornography-and-the-church/. "15 Mind-Blowing Statistics about Pornography and the Church." Mission Frontiers. Accessed May 21, 2023. https://www.missionfrontiers.org/issue/article/15-mind-blowing-statistics-about-pornography-and-the-church.

3. Artemis as asia minor mother goddess from a statue in the Vatican ... Accessed May 21, 2023. https://www.researchgate.net/figure/Artemis-as-Asia-Minor-mother-goddess-from-a-statue-in-the-Vatican-Museum-The-egg-shaped_fig3_339615583.

4. "Egeria." Encyclopædia Britannica. Accessed May 21, 2023. https://www.britannica.com/topic/Egeria.

5. "Diana." Encyclopædia Britannica. Accessed May 21, 2023. https://www.britannica.com/topic/Diana-Roman-religion.

6. Ndongala , Gloire. A Roaring Lion, an Angel of Light, n.d.

7. Strongs's #3823: Pale - greek/hebrew definitions - bible tools. Accessed May 21, 2023.

https://www.bibletools.org/index.cfm/fuseaction/Lexicon.show/ID/G3823/pale.htm.

8. Strong's Greek: 746. ἀρχή (Arché) -- beginning, origin. Accessed May 21, 2023. https://biblehub.com/greek/746.htm.

9. Strong's Hebrew: 8269. שַׂר (SAR) -- chieftain, chief, ruler, official, captain, prince. Accessed May 21, 2023. https://biblehub.com/hebrew/8269.htm.

10. "Map of the Persian Empire." Bible History. Accessed May 21, 2023. https://bible-history.com/maps/persian-empire.

11. "Baal." Encyclopædia Britannica, March 29, 2023. https://www.britannica.com/topic/Baal-ancient-deity.

12. White, Ellen. "Asherah and the Asherim: Goddess or Cult Symbol? - Biblical Archaeology Society." Biblical Archaeology Society -, August 6, 2022. https://www.biblicalarchaeology.org/daily/ancient-cultures/ancient-israel/asherah-and-the-asherim-goddess-or-cult-symbol/.

13. Strongs's #1849: Exousia - Greek/Hebrew definitions - bible tools. Accessed May 21, 2023. https://www.bibletools.org/index.cfm/fuseaction/Lexicon.show/ID/G1849/exousia.htm.

14. Daniel 7:25. Accessed May 21, 2023. https://biblehub.com/commentaries/daniel/7-25.htm.

15. Strong's greek: 5293. ὑποτάσσω (hupotassó) -- to place or rank under, to subject, mid. to obey. Accessed May 21, 2023. https://biblehub.com/greek/5293.htm.

16. Strong's greek: 436. ἀνθίστημι (anthistémi) -- to set against, i.e. withstand. Accessed May 21, 2023. https://biblehub.com/greek/436.htm.

17. Staff, BibleStudyTools. "Colossians 2:15." biblestudytools.com. Accessed May 21, 2023. https://www.biblestudytools.com/colossians/2-15.html?amp.

18. "Bill Mounce." ἐπιτιμάω. Accessed May 21, 2023. https://www.billmounce.com/greek-dictionary/epitimao.

19. "Enduring Word Bible Commentary Luke Chapter 8." Enduring Word, March 15, 2023. https://enduringword.com/bible-commentary/luke-8/amp/.

20. Webmaster, The. "The Greco-Roman World." History of Christian Theology, August 17, 2022. https://historyofchristiantheology.com/commentary/period-i-early-and-medieval-church/greco-roman-world/.

21. GotQuestions.org. "Maccabean Revolt." GotQuestions.org, October 9, 2018. https://www.gotquestions.org/Maccabean-Revolt.html.

22. “The Roman Army.” English History, December 2, 2022. https://englishhistory.net/romans/the-roman-army/.

23. “Mark 5 Commentary - Matthew Henry Commentary on the Whole Bible (Complete).” biblestudytools.com. Accessed May 21, 2023. https://www.biblestudytools.com/commentaries/matthew-henry-complete/mark/5.html.

24. “Praetor Definition & Meaning.” Merriam-Webster. Accessed May 21, 2023. https://www.merriam-webster.com/dictionary/praetor.

25. “Consul.” Encyclopædia Britannica. Accessed May 21, 2023. https://www.britannica.com/topic/consul-ancient-Roman-official.

26. “Enduring Word Bible Commentary Ephesians Chapter 6.” Enduring Word, March 16, 2023. https://enduringword.com/bible-commentary/ephesians-6/.

27. Strong’s greek: 2888. κοσμοκράτωρ (Kosmokratór) -- a ruler of this world. Accessed May 21, 2023. https://biblehub.com/greek/2888.htm.

28. “World - Kosmos (Greek Word Study).” Precept Austin. Accessed May 21, 2023. https://www.preceptaustin.org/world-kosmos.

29. Strong’s greek: 2902. κρατέω (krateó) -- to be strong, rule. Accessed May 21, 2023. https://biblehub.com/greek/2902.htm.

30. STEP. Accessed May 21, 2023. https://www.stepbible.org/?q=version&options=VHNUG.

31. Strong's Greek: 4189. πονηρία (ponéria) -- iniquity. Accessed May 21, 2023. https://www.biblehub.com/greek/4189.htm.

32. "Ponos." Greek Mythology. Accessed May 21, 2023. https://www.greekmythology.com/Other_Gods/Minor_Gods/Ponos/ponos.html#:~:text=Ponos%20was%20the%20god%20of,Nyx%2C%20the%20goddess%20of%20night.

33. Strong's greek: 2616. καταδυναστεύω (katadunasteuo) -- I overpower, quell, treat harshly. Accessed May 21, 2023. https://biblehub.com/greek/2616.htm.

34. "Synonymous Parallelism." Encyclopædia Britannica. Accessed May 21, 2023. https://www.britannica.com/topic/synonymous-parallelism.

35. What the Bible says about Bene Ha Elohim. Accessed May 21, 2023. https://www.bibletools.org/index.cfm/fuseaction/Topical.show/RTD/cgg/ID/23558/Bene-Ha-Elohim.htm.

36. "Rephaim , Emim and Zamzummim : The Hebrew Meaning of the Mysterious Ancient Nation of Giants." hebrewversity, February 7, 2021. https://www.hebrewversity.com/rephaim-emim-zamzummim-hebrew-meaning-mysterious-ancient-nation-giants/.

37. Donnelly, Deirdre E, and Patrick J Morrison. "Hereditary Gigantism-the Biblical Giant Goliath and His Brothers." The Ulster medical journal, May 2014. https://www.ncbi.nlm.nih.gov/pmc/articles/PMC4113151/.

38. Abarim Publications. “The Amazing Name Rephaim: Meaning and Etymology.” Abarim Publications. Accessed May 22, 2023. https://www.abarim-publications.com/Meaning/Rephaim.html.

39. “A Nation of Giants – Who Were the Rephaim?” hebrewversity, November 12, 2022. https://www.hebrewversity.com/nation-giants-rephaim/.

40. How to Say Ghost in Hebrew. Accessed May 22, 2023. https://ulpan.com/say-ghost-hebrew-special-post-yom-hashoah/).

41. Staff, BibleStudyTools. “1 Corinthians 11:10.” biblestudytools.com. Accessed May 22, 2023. https://www.biblestudytools.com/1-corinthians/11-10.html.

42. Lumpkin, Joseph B. The books of Enoch: The angels, the Watchers and the Nephilim, with extensive commentary on the three books of Enoch, The fallen angels, the calendar of enoch, and daniel’s prophecy. Blountsville, AL: Fifth Estate Publishers, 2015.

43. Proverbs 9:18 commentaries. Accessed May 22, 2023. https://biblehub.com/commentaries/proverbs/9-18.htm.

44. “Nymph.” Encyclopædia Britannica, May 11, 2023. https://www.britannica.com/topic/nymph-Greek-mythology.

45. “Hermaphroditos.” HERMAPHRODITUS (Hermaphroditos) - Greek God of Hermaphrodites & Effeminates. Accessed May 22, 2023. https://www.theoi.com/Ouranios/ErosHermaphroditos.html.

46. Reeves, Ryan. “What Is the Septuagint?” The Gospel Coalition (TGC). Accessed May 22, 2023. https://www.thegospelcoalition.org/article/what-is-the-septuagint/?amp.

47. “Is Lilith Just a Mythical Monster, or Is There Any Biblical Truth?” biblestudytools.com, May 17, 2023. https://www.biblestudytools.com/bible-study/topical-studies/is-lilith-just-a-mythical-monster-or-is-there-any-biblical-truth.html.

48. Bolinger, Hope. “What Is a Succubus and Is It Mentioned in the Bible?” Christianity, November 14, 2022. https://www.christianity.com/wiki/angels-and-demons/succubus-bible.html?amp=1.

49. “Isaiah 13:21 - Καὶ Ἀναπαύσονται... - Interlinear Study Bible.” StudyLight.org. Accessed May 22, 2023. https://www.studylight.org/interlinear-study-bible/greek/isaiah/13-21.html.

50. “Enduring Word Bible Commentary Isaiah Chapter 13.” Enduring Word, March 10, 2023. https://enduringword.com/bible-commentary/isaiah-13/.

51. Cartwright, Mark. “Satyr.” World History Encyclopedia, March 29, 2023. https://www.worldhistory.org/satyr/.

52. Lockett, Rachel. "Satyrs: Animal Spirits of Ancient Greece." History Cooperative, August 9, 2022. https://historycooperative.org/satyrs/#:~:text=Satyrs%20are%20believed%20to%20represent,characteristics%20of%20goats%20or%20horses

53. "2. Caesarea Philippi (Banias)-from the God Pan to the God-Man." 2. Caesarea Philippi (Banias)-From The God Pan To The God-Man | Bible.org. Accessed May 22, 2023. https://bible.org/seriespage/2-caesarea-philippi-banias-god-pan-god-man.

54. "Day 8 - Mt. Hermon, Tel Dan, Banias Falls, Caesarea Philippi, Hogoshrim." Biblos Foundation, March 17, 2018. https://www.biblosfoundation.org/tour/day-8-day-8-mt-hermon-tel-dan-banias-falls-caesarea-philippi-hogoshrim/.

55. "Mermaid." Encyclopædia Britannica, May 17, 2023. https://www.britannica.com/topic/mermaid.

56. "11 Egyptian Gods and Goddesses." Encyclopædia Britannica. Accessed May 22, 2023. https://www.britannica.com/list/11-egyptian-gods-and-goddesses.

57. "Dagan." Encyclopædia Britannica, April 15, 2023. https://www.britannica.com/topic/Dagan.

58. "Judges 16:4." BibleRef.com. Accessed May 22, 2023. https://www.bibleref.com/Judges/16/Judges-16-4.html.

59. GotQuestions.org. "Chemosh." GotQuestions.org, May 13, 2015. https://www.gotquestions.org/who-Chemosh.html.

60. "Leviathan Spirit - Characteristics and How to Fight It." biblestudytools.com, November 15, 2021. https://www.biblestudytools.com/bible-study/topical-studies/what-is-a-leviathan-spirit-and-how-can-you-identify-it.html.

61. "Leviathan." Encyclopædia Britannica. Accessed May 22, 2023. https://www.britannica.com/topic/Leviathan-Middle-Eastern-mythology.

62. "The Amazing Name Jezebel: Meaning and Etymology." Abarim Publications, www.abarim-publications.com/Meaning/Jezebel.html. Accessed 22 May 2023.

63. Abarim Publications. "The Amazing Name Ethbaal: Meaning and Etymology." Abarim Publications. Accessed May 22, 2023. https://www.abarim-publications.com/Meaning/Ethbaal.html

64. "Enduring Word Bible Commentary Revelation Chapter 2." Enduring Word, March 16, 2023. https://enduringword.com/bible-commentary/revelation-2/.

65. "Spirit of Divination." SPIRIT OF DIVINATION - The Spirit Of Python Of Delphi. Accessed May 22, 2023. https://www.bibleversestudy.com/acts/acts16-spirit-of-divination.htm.

66. "Lesson 2: The Belt of Truth." Free Bible Study Guides. Accessed May 22, 2023. http://www.freebiblestudyguides.org/bible-teachings/armor-of-god-belt-of-truth.htm.

67. "Enduring Word Bible Commentary Revelation Chapter 2." Enduring Word, March 16, 2023. https://enduringword.com/bible-commentary/revelation-2/.

68. "Enduring Word Bible Commentary Ephesians Chapter 6." Enduring Word, March 16, 2023. https://enduringword.com/bible-commentary/ephesians-6/.

69. Valeii, Kathi. "How Does Intergenerational Trauma Work?" Verywell Health, September 4, 2021. https://www.verywellhealth.com/intergenerational-trauma-5191638#:~:text=Intergenerational%20trauma%20is%20the%20theory,gene%20functions%20(epigenetic%20change).

70. Staff, BibleStudyTools. "Genesis 25:21 - Isaac Prayed to the Lord on Behalf of His Wife, Be..." biblestudytools.com. Accessed May 22, 2023. https://www.biblestudytools.com/genesis/25-21.html#:~:text=Genesis%2025%3A21%20in%20Other%20Translations&text=21%20Isaac%20pleaded%20with%20the,Rebekah%20became%20pregnant%20with%20twins.&text=21%20Isaac%20prayed%20hard%20to,wife%20because%20she%20was%20barren.

www.ingramcontent.com/pod-product-compliance
Lightning Source LLC
LaVergne TN
LVHW081259100826
845148LV00005B/919

* 9 7 9 8 9 8 5 6 4 7 3 8 9 *